NO WONDER MY PARENTS DRANK

 Tales from a Stand-Up Dad

JAY MOHR

Simon & Schuster Paperbacks

New York   London   Toronto   Sydney

Simon & Schuster Paperbacks
A Division of Simon & Schuster, Inc.
1230 Avenue of the Americas
New York, NY 10020

First Simon & Schuster trade paperback edition May 2011

SIMON & SCHUSTER PAPERBACKS and colophon are registered
trademarks of Simon & Schuster, Inc.

For information about special discounts for bulk purchases,
please contact Simon & Schuster Special Sales at
1-866-506-1949 or business@simonandschuster.com.

The Simon & Schuster Speakers Bureau can bring authors
to your live event. For more information or to book an event,
contact the Simon & Schuster Speakers Bureau at
1-866-248-3049 or visit our website at www.simonspeakers.com.

Designed by Nancy Singer

Manufactured in the United States of America

10   9   8   7   6   5   4   3   2   1

The Library of Congress has cataloged the the hardcover edition as follows:

Mohr, Jay.
    No wonder my parents drank : tales from a stand-up dad / Jay Mohr.
p.   cm.
1. Fatherhood—Humor. 2. Parenting—Humor. I. Title.
    PN6231.F37M65 2010
    306.874'20207—dc22   2009051614

ISBN 978-1-4391-7321-3
ISBN 978-1-4391-7322-0 (pbk)
ISBN 978-1-4391-7323-7 (ebook)

For

Nicole Avery Cox Mohr,

my baby bride.

My wife, my life, my light . . .

". . . not even the rain."

CONTENTS

CONTENTS

Buddy Hackett: "Why do grandparents and grandchildren have such a special bond?"

Buddy Hackett's rabbi: "Common enemy."

"Want to know how much it costs to have a kid? All of it."

—*Ron Bennington*

"If you were my kid, I'd leave you at a night game."

—*Joe Mantegna to Jay Mohr*

NO
WONDER
MY
PARENTS
DRANK

THE BIG TOP

Being a parent is like going to the circus.

Being a parent is like joining the circus.

Being a parent is like becoming the *ringmaster* of the circus. It sweeps into town, bringing with it much fanfare and excitement—and ready or not, you are in charge.

There will be loud noises. Somebody will cry. A lot. There will be animals. Some you will train and love and eventually they will get flushed down the toilet or buried in the backyard. Some will be taken to the vet, never to return. There will be acrobats. Sometimes your tiny performers will jump off the couch and bust their forehead and need a couple of stitches. Sometimes

1

they will go flying off backward from a moving swing and land in a heap. You will hold your breath. Your knuckles will be white. You'll panic and you will run to them—only for this daredevil to jump up and smile. You will applaud. You will have bearded ladies. (The beards will be bubbles and they will be in the tub but it is still a freak show.) There will be sticky foods and tummy aches and somebody will throw up.

There will be odd smells—some wonderful (the popcorn; the little fried doughnuts; the sweet, indescribable smell of sweaty hair after a midday nap, so familiar and so foreign and so perfect that applying any adjectives is a fool's errand) and others awful (potty training—no need to elaborate).

Somebody will cry. A lot.

There will be endless lines to wait in. Lines at the rides, lines at the restrooms. There will be lines at the pediatrician's office. There will be music so loud and colors so bright and exhaustion so bone-crushing and you'll know everything in your circus would run so much more smoothly if everyone could *just get a little more sleep.* They won't.

There will be clowns. They will be strange and their faces will be covered with paint and no matter what doctor-preferred product you use, the paint just won't come off. You will drive a clown car. You will wonder how it will be humanly possible to fit the car seats and the diaper bags and the juice boxes and the people and the pets into one vehicle. Somehow you will.

Sometimes it will be scary. The dog is old and cranky and

your tiny lion tamer just might get bit. There will be fevers and colic and bee stings that swell up and it will be three in the morning and you will be wondering, Where are all the grown-ups? Then you will remember that the grown-up is you. YOU are the ringmaster and you don't even have the tall silk hat.

Somebody will cry. A lot.

Sometimes it will be joyous. You will laugh so hard you shake. You will stare wide-eyed as magic tricks are performed right in front of you. They say your name for the first time. They take their first steps. They write your name the first time. They learn to run. Toward you, they run. They know you will catch them. Eventually they will run to others.

It will be expensive. No matter how much cash you have, it is never enough. It's not enough for the T-shirts and the braces, the refreshments and the math tutors. It's not enough for the poorly made stuffed animals that they *have* to have and soon forget. It's not enough for picture day and piano lessons and cotton candy and college.

Much like the circus, being a parent seems to be going out of style. I don't mean the celebrity "bump watch," fancy baby shower kind of parents. I am talking about the good old-fashioned, hands in the dirt, covered in spit kind of parents. We are all so busy with our lives and our BlackBerrys and our hybrid cars and our organic diets and our jobs, our jobs, our jobs.

We have to slow down at least a little. I know I do.

Pretty soon the circus packs up and leaves town. Sure, we'll have pictures. And they will come and visit at Thanksgiving. But mostly you will have the quiet. You will hear the music and laughter in the distance on some faraway backyard, but for you the circus has moved on and there's just one big empty space where the Ferris wheel and the high chair used to be. How could all of those endless years have flown by in an eyelash's flutter? Why was I in such a hurry? Where did it all go? This "Greatest Show on Earth"? Why did I ever complain? I liked being the ringmaster and I never really cared much for hats anyway.

I just saw my son's cobweb-covered car seat in the garage, put away for another day, another child.

I cried. A lot. I'm going back. I miss the circus.

Let me explain.

1

ESCALATING LOVE

My father was a quiet, aloof man. The combination of these two characteristics always gave me the feeling that he simply didn't like me. In retrospect, I was absolutely bat-shit as a child. My dad's aloofness was surely nothing more than a defense mechanism to keep from having me taken away to a boarding school in Switzerland. If my father paid any more attention to me than he already did, he would have had to have his ears removed. I know that my father loves me deeply and unconditionally. When I was a kid, he just didn't say it a lot. Not many dads do. Like many, if not most fathers of his generation, my dad was not an "I love you" type of guy. He would say it back to me occasionally if I said it first but the whole process made him uncomfortable. As a child, I hated him for this. As an adult, I realize now that he was a product of the way his father had treated him, and the way my grandfather was treated by his father.

If you go far enough back in your family's history and look high enough up into your family tree, I feel that most of us fathers today would discover the same thing. Love escalates. The longer you look back at the relationships between fathers and their children, the less amount of outward love you can see expressed. How much time do you think your great-great-grandfather spent telling his kids he loved them? My theory is he gave a little bit more than he received as a child and that's it. I imagine that the Great Depression probably stripped them of their pride and tenderness and they rarely, if ever, locked eyes with their child, held them by the hand, and said "I love you so much!" The world has obviously changed quite a bit and plenty of time could be spent debating whether it is for better or worse. Some would say that times were so much simpler back then. Maybe. But I truly believe that we are entering the most wonderful era of life in our nation's history.

My theory of "escalating love" gives me great hope when I look at the world around me. Regardless of what terrible things are reported in the papers or on the news at night, I know that like many fathers of this generation, I *am* an "I love you" type of guy. The friends I have are also quick to tell their children they love them. I see it at the malls and in the park, too.

When I was growing up, there were never any fathers at

the park. If someone's father was at the park, it usually meant someone was in trouble. Not anymore, my friend. Dads go to parks these days and while we are at the parks we play and we play hard. We love hard. We are the first generation of "I love you" dads. Our children will be the first generation to grow up en masse in this environment and the love we share with our children today will *escalate* upward to their children and so on. Pretty neat, huh?

My son, Jackson, was born on September 27, 2002. Like me, he was born at four-thirty in the afternoon. Like me, he was also two and a half months premature. Jackie wasn't supposed to be born until December 15, 2002. You can call it cosmic, you can call it coincidence. I call it misery. There is nothing like spending a month in the neonatal intensive care unit at your local hospital. I was much sicker as a newborn than Jackie was. I had many different lung ailments and I've had regular bouts with bronchitis and pneumonia my entire life. Jackie had no illnesses; he just arrived very early. Also unlike me, he arrived via C-section. I was in the delivery room to witness the birth. I was a vaginal birth and what they call breech, which means feet first. I hadn't been a textbook breech birth because I was actually born butt first. My head and toes were touching inside my mother's birth canal and I had to be gingerly pulled out by my ass. Not only was I myself early, but I also set the tone for my childhood early. The first memory anyone has of me is my asshole. I always knew how to make an entrance.

A C-section is a bizarre thing to witness. I have never seen a vaginal birth, so I have nothing to compare it to, but the entire thing seemed pretty anticlimactic. It was a bit like pulling a sea bass out of the ocean. The doctor made a neat incision across the belly and after some rooting around, Jackie breached the skin line. He looked like an Olympic swimmer. His right arm and head came out simultaneously as if he were taking a breath during the freestyle relay.

When the doctor pulled him from the womb and held him aloft, it wasn't a sight for the weak of stomach. My boy was covered in blood and a film of white custard. If you are a father then you will believe me that it was the single most beautiful thing I ever saw in my life. It *was* life! God made man and I made my child. The room faded away around me. I was stunned by the sight of him. He looked like everyone I had ever known. He looked like my father. He looked like his parents and our parents and all the cousins we ever had. For months I had wondered what my child would look like. I spent days musing over whether he would have blond hair or brown or red. I wondered what his facial structure would be. Would he have a button nose? How big a chin would he have? As I watched television during the pregnancy, my mind would wander after particular faces appeared. Would he look like that guy? How about him? What about that guy's red hair but this guy's cheekbones? I rolled every composite imaginable around in my head, anticipating his birth. When he was born, I would finally be able to put a face to the name. The moment Jackie arrived, I thought, Of course that's what he looks like. I have spoken with other fathers about this, and it seems to be a common thought. My son looked like himself. The first and only boy of his kind. There is a tender and almost ethereal moment when, after looking at your newborn child, you realize he actually looks *familiar*. Everything I am describing to you took place in a matter of three, maybe four seconds. It seemed like I stood staring at my son with everyone else frozen around us for hours and hours. I will remember and cherish the memory of that moment for the rest of my life, so in the end I guess it lasted much longer than hours and hours.

I was pulled from my reverie when it dawned on me that out of all the sounds I was hearing, my newborn child's cry was not one of them. I heard the doctor quietly instructing another doctor and some nurses as to what to do next and where to do it. I heard many voices and the hum of the machines in the delivery room. I heard my own heart beat in my head. The omission of his cries, however, was deafening. Waiting to be sure your child is breathing is a long, torturous affair. The tension was magnified exponentially by the fact that Jackson was born ten weeks earlier than he was scheduled to arrive. But eventually, finally, I heard the most beautiful sound I had heard up to that point in my life. I heard a loud and long wail coming from my boy. I exhaled and almost fainted at the same time. The OB-GYN made a cute joke by counting Jackie's fingers and toes out loud. He started with his tiny tree frog–looking fingers: ". . . eight, nine, ten." He then held my child aloft and counted the smallest toes imaginable: ". . . seven, eight, nine, ten." Then "Looks good from here!" With that proclamation he carried Jackie over to a small table to my left to weigh him and measure him. Obviously, having arrived as early as he did, he was small. He was seventeen and a half inches and weighed in at a less-than-massive three pounds. It didn't matter to me if he was one inch and one pound. He was finally here. And he was perfect.

After clearing the infant's throat and checking a few vital signs, the doctor handed me a pair of scissors and said simply, "Ready?" I was about to cut my son's umbilical cord and no one had ever prepared me or explained how to do it. As I took his former lifeline in my hands, I wondered just how badly I could screw this up: For all intents and purposes I believed I was about to shape his belly button for the rest of his life. What if I cut it too close to the skin and he gets horrible pains as he gains weight? What if I cut too little and my poor kid has to walk around for the rest of his life with a four-inch flap of skin dangling from his belly like a little tail? I am proud to say that I cut perfectly, and Jackie's belly button will render you helpless to not give him a raspberry on his stomach if you see it. (Until he gets older, and then I'll have to call the cops.)

After the cord was cut and his body was cleaned and measured, my child was simply taken away. Not much was said by way of explanation. I knew that due to his prematurity he would not be coming home from the hospital for a while but nothing prepared me for the vacuum I felt in my heart as people with masks and slip-on booties over their shoes simply and matter-of-factly took him from the room. Where were they taking him? When would I see him again? Would I see him again? I would, but his new environment wouldn't be as pleasant as I would have liked.

If you have never set foot in a neonatal intensive care unit, consider yourself very, very fortunate. Because of the serious-ness and dreadfulness of Jackson's surroundings, I became completely numb as to what was happening around me. Each day and night, as I pulled my truck into the hospital's parking garage, I would systematically desensitize myself to everything in life that wasn't his sweet heartbeat. I no longer saw people's faces or clothing. I managed to not hear anything other than the soft "bing bong" of my son's monitors and I absolutely never, ever looked into the first two bays of babies, who were there because of the overwhelmingly sad fact that they were most likely never coming home. I couldn't allow myself any stimuli whatsoever. I rationalized that if I allowed myself to see what was going wrong with other infants, I would be allowing myself to look over the edge of a cliff called doubt. As far as I was con-cerned, Jackie was the only thing in that hospital. Looking back, I am not sure how I didn't walk into walls or bump into passersby. Once, I was sitting at Jackson's incubator and a nurse was giving various instructions on how to care for the baby without interfering with all of his tubes. This was a monumental moment because it meant that he was healthy enough to be lifted out of his incubator and be held outside of it for a half hour or so at a time. I listened so closely and so intensely. I knew the importance of this moment and wanted to be sure to take the most precious care while handling my child. After about twenty minutes, Jackie and I were alone. I lifted him gingerly from his glass house and secured his blankets to make sure he stayed warm and gathered him into my arms. He looked utterly and perfectly serene as we did the parent-child dance for the first time. A few moments later, a doctor poked his head in and asked me about the nurse who had just walked out of the room moments before. He asked if the nurse did certain tests or administered something or other. I froze. Nurse? What nurse? What is a nurse? All I know is baby, this baby. The unfazed doctor explained that the nurse that just left did a routine check and he now wanted to have a look at Jackie's chart. I looked around the curtain and saw two nurses standing five feet from me. One was thin and white; the other was obese and black. I hadn't the slightest idea as to which of these two nurses was standing in front of me no more than thirty seconds ago. The doctor thought I was being a wiseass and I tried to explain my position. "You don't understand," I pleaded. "I am not here." I was physically at the hospital but mentally I was long, long gone. I went to that hospital to see one heart beat on one monitor and that was it. No nurses lived, no doctors or patients existed, just my child—the most beautiful boy in the world. If I allowed myself to be aware of what and who was around me, I would have been crippled with terror. If I saw the babies under the bright lights or the sobbing parents or the hushed consultations between doctors and dads, I would have been allowing myself to realize the countless number of things that could at any moment go terribly wrong. I didn't wish to know why babies wore tiny sunglasses and sat under blinding sunlamps. I couldn't have my brain process why incubators that were occupied yesterday were empty today.

I know today, by looking back into my subconscious, what was happening inside the walls of the NICU that autumn. At the time, however, I held strongly a belief that I hold strongly to this day: You cannot have fear and faith at the same time. The ultimate test of faith for me at that time was waiting day after day for a doctor to give my son his walking papers. Until that day came, I put all my eggs in the faith basket. Everything was fine and would continue to be fine because it was fine. Period. I didn't trust myself to let any visual doubt or questions enter into my head. I highly recommend this approach to any parents who finds themselves in a NICU waiting for their child to come home. Everything is fine and will continue to be fine because it is fine. Say it to yourself over and over until you go mad and then come back again. It will be fine. I assure you. Eventually, Jackson slept peacefully ten feet from me in his bedroom. The worries of whether his feeding tube was straight were quickly replaced by worries of whether he would wake up with a diaper full of poop and then whether he would choke on a piece of new food that I didn't cut small enough and now whether he will fall off the monkey bars during recess and break his leg. These new worries are nothing short of divine.

Oddly, Jackson's cries became a very soothing sound while he was in the NICU. It meant he was alive and pissed off about something. I would tell my parents this discovery, and trying to be funny or forbearing they would be quick to quip, "Oh yeah? You just wait until you get him home!" I was proudly and eagerly waiting.

As parents we try as hard as humanly possible to give our children whatever it is we didn't have. We overextend ourselves to be sure our kids are saturated in whatever it is we feel we were lacking. At the end of the day we all learn pretty much the same lesson: Our parents did the best they could with what they had. I know there are obvious exceptions but for the most part I believe this is true. As sure as you are reading this, I am certain that Jackson, despite my best efforts, will find something in my parenting to complain about. This is incredible to imagine because I think I am doing a near perfect job. Seriously, Jackie has a huge set of balls if he complains. Most of the mistakes I have made happened before he was two years old and I have rewritten history and convinced him that they never happened. My son knows I have never spanked him. My child is confident that he is completely safe with me and I never, ever pulled out of the driveway without fastening his seat belt. I never slept through his crying. I never let him cry alone in a room for an hour straight. I never walked outside to get the mail, leaving my boy to crawl around the house unsupervised. I never put him in the overhead storage bin on a flight from LAX to San Jose. (Well, I never forgot him there.) I never did these things and neither did you. That's our story and we'll stick to it until our children have children.

Having a child is like being born again. All the colors in the world are brighter. Everything is significant. Nothing is too small to notice or enjoy. You begin to find pleasure in the tiniest details. You obsess over how soft your baby's blanket is. You will wonder how long anchors and nautical themes have been on baby boys' pajamas. These are all things you never could have noticed before a baby moved into your house. Our entire lives, we have woken up in the morning and thought about what we will do with ourselves. When baby comes home from the hospital, you don't even make it through the night. You wake up to pee at three in the morning and you start planning out great things to do with your baby when the sun comes up. Oddly, it never dawns on us that our child will remember none of it. How many people do you know who can tell you about a great trip to the museum they had as a baby? None! We plan entire days around the entertainment of a freaking baby! Do we even know if the baby has a good time? They've never told us. We've never gotten a chubby thumbs-up. None of us have had our three-year-old son thank us for the trip to the Spaghetti Factory when he was three months old. And yet we keep filling our days with things to pleasure our babies. We even take our babies on vacation with us. That is really the absolute dumbest thing we do. My wife, Nik, and I are guilty of this. Jackie had been to Hawaii three times before he turned six. He has no real memory of it. The kayak rides, the snorkeling, the little kid surfboard lessons, Santa Claus surfing onto the beach and handing out candy to everyone are all things he has no memory of happening. Then why the hell was it such a great idea at the time? I even took Jackie with Nik and me to meet soldiers at Pearl Harbor on the Fourth of July. We rode together on the captain's barge. The seamen saluted our boy when he got on and off the barge. We saw fireworks and went to a luau. When I ask him about it now, he straight-faces me. He wants to remember it all. When I explain it to him it sounds incredible. Sadly, he has no idea what I am talking about. He is seven. In two years, Jackie's memory has been wiped clean of everything we have done for him. The flowers placed around his neck at the airport and the hula dancers have been replaced by Pokémon and SpongeBob dialogue.

Here is my first word of advice in this book. Don't do anything expensive with your kids until they are at least eight. You will save thousands of dollars, too! Don't take the baby with you to Manhattan. The baby won't miss it and you will pad your bank account with an extra five grand for the week. Go on that cruise, just you and your wife alone. You won't have to pay for at-sea day care and you will have a lot more sex. Even when our children enjoy a vacation or a big activity, they always seem to enjoy the wrong parts of it. Nik and I were somehow lucky enough to become friends with the curator of the Los Angeles Zoo. With this friendship came an awesome perk. We could go to the zoo pretty much whenever we wanted and have someone drive us around on a golf cart and let us feed the animals. One morning, we all went to the zoo and walked into the giraffe exhibit and hand-fed them long strips of leaves. We even got to feed the baby giraffe a bottle of milk. Jackie stretched his arms up as far as they would go and the baby giraffe hung his head down low to suckle at the nipple Jackie was holding four feet off the ground.

To this day, if you ask Jackie if he has ever been to the zoo, he will tell you that he has been to the zoo and at the zoo they have toilets that flush by themselves. That's what my son remembers about hand-feeding giraffes. That when he took a piss, the toilet flushed itself.

Some of the trash cans at the zoo have faces painted on them, so that the trash goes in the "animal"'s mouth. Minutes after feeding a Sumatran rhino heads of lettuce by hand, my son yelled out, "Daddy, look! I'm feeding the trash can!" The kid just gave lettuce to a rhino and here he was stuffing a paper bag into a trash can. He was laughing maniacally like he could not believe that any boy on earth could be as lucky as he, because he was feeding a trash can. I thought that maybe he was "special." He's not. He is quite normal. He was acting like all kids act. Unpredictably.

When we have children, we too begin to act unpredictably. We find ourselves doing things we never thought we would do. Like take walks. We start talking to the neighbors. We start taking life a little more slowly. When we walk with our babies, we don't have a destination. We just walk. When we pass people on the street we say hello and make a little pleasant small talk. We notice if a breeze is blowing. We smell the star jasmine and we notice when the temperature changes five degrees.

One day, I was walking Jackie around the block in his stroller (which of course he doesn't remember). As we came up a small stretch of hill on my street, I noticed my neighbor had the most enormous red roses growing on her lawn. I wheeled the stroller up to the roses and bent one down toward Jackie's face so he could smell it. He took a good healthy whiff and then I filled my face with the incredible aroma. Over my shoulder I noticed the sound of a piano. My neighbor was inside her house playing. I had never really spoken with this neighbor and I never knew that she played an instrument. At this particular moment, my neighbor was playing a marvelous piece. Her windows were screened for the summer and the sound spilled out into the warm air. I stood there stunned at the beautiful music surrounding me. I watched Jackie reach up for another hit off the rose and I started to cry. I cried a lot. I was completely overwhelmed by the sound, the smell, and the sight of my afternoon. These are all things that I would have overlooked had I not been with my child. I wiped my eyes and got my act together and pushed the stroller home. Once inside my house I wrote my neighbor an anonymous note, thanking her for her gift of music and roses that day.

What kind of a homo has this baby turned me into? Suddenly I am crying in public, literally stopping to smell the roses, and writing thank-you notes? Wow, this kid put a whammy on me. It would prove to be the greatest and most frustrating whammy in the world.

The most amazing things happen when you have kids. Conversely, the strangest and most aggravating things happen when you have kids. Your sleep goes right out the window. You stop hanging out with all of your friends. You stop swearing and drinking and partying (hopefully). For years people have used the expression "the old ball and chain" to refer to wives. I think wives have gotten a bad rap. At least with a wife you can attempt to use logic and explain why it is important for you to go to a concert or a Dodgers game. You cannot rationalize your whereabouts to a baby. They are the real ball and chains. If you have a baby, chances are you aren't going to whatever it is you were just invited to. If you do decide to go, you will be so weighed down by baby gear and backpacks with milk in them that you will feel like a complete jackass the second you get there. You will also realize that being home with your baby and watching reruns of *Law & Order* is about as much fun as all the old stuff you used to do anyway.

I tell my son I love him many times each day. When my son says it to me first, it stops me dead in my tracks and I swoon. What a privilege it is to be a father. A child tells me he loves me every day! You and I have the capacity—the duty, really—to give our children everything we feel we didn't get enough of growing up. So let me say to you: If you're a father, congratulations. You have just been let in on the most precious secret and the most joyous thing this world has to offer.

I promise you the rest of this book will be much funnier. I just had to first unite those of us out there who find parenting a bit overwhelming. And isn't that every parent? Think of this book as an AA meeting for parents. We all realize we are powerless over our children and the hours they keep. We realize we need a power greater than us to restore our sanity. We will take a fearless inventory of ourselves. We will say we are sorry a lot. My name is Jay and I am a parent.

2

PREPARING FOR BABY

Webster's Dictionary defines *prepare* as "to put in proper condition or readiness."

Readiness? I didn't even know that *readiness* was a word. But who am I to argue with Webster? What I can say with complete confidence, though, is that saying that you can be "ready" for a baby is like saying that you can be "ready" for a natural disaster. We know that things are going to get shaken up, we know we'll be out of our element and there are supplies to be had. But really, how the hell does one "prepare" for his life to be turned completely upside down?

I wasn't ready for my son to be born three months premature. To be honest, I wasn't ready for him at all. I was a lout. I was a loudmouthed know-it-all who always had to have things go my way. The thought of me being in charge of another human being's welfare was laughable. Well, it would have been laughable if it didn't happen to me at four-thirty in the afternoon that fall day. What had once been laughable became instantly terrifying. I had no idea how to be a father. I had no idea how to do laundry or how to mix formula or how to install a car seat. I was clueless about how to change a diaper. I didn't know how to soothe a grown-up, let alone a baby. I couldn't even find the remote. Parenthood is probably best described by the old expression "If you want God to laugh, make plans." I quickly learned that when it comes to parenthood there should be a change in that expression: "If you want God to laugh, have expectations."

I'm not sure what I expected when I became a father but I do know that every day for the next seven years, my expectations and hopes would be blown out of the water daily. I am sure that if you are a parent and reading this, you are solemnly nodding your head in agreement. Having kids is like Murphy's law taking place every day inside your heart. If you want your son to be an athlete, he will become a total spaz. If you want your daughter to be a beauty queen, she will be cross-eyed. If your wish is for your daughter to go out into the world and get a great education, she will be as dumb as a bag of hair. Parents make big plans and God laughs. Every day. You go to sleep at night and think up a big plan to take your daughter to the beach. You can hardly sleep because of how excited you are that you thought of something so cool for your kid. You reflect back on all the times you wish your parents had taken you to the beach, and you lie in the dark and silently gloat that you are going to be a better parent than your parents ever were. Then you wake up in the morning and tell your daughter the big, huge, wonderful beach news and she looks you in the eye and says, "I don't want to go to the beach." You stand there stunned while holding towels and wearing white shit on your nose. You think, Who the fuck doesn't want to go to the beach? Your child doesn't want to go to the beach because you planned a day at the beach. Welcome aboard.

So we've established that the moment Jackie was released from the womb, I realized—in a moment of simultaneous bliss and sheer terror—that I could never be mentally prepared for the event. But let's call a spade a spade (where did that expression come from anyway?): my lack of "readiness" for my child began months before his birth . . . when I realized that I had to liter-ally and physically *prepare* for his arrival. For the slow audience and the cheap seats, this means that I had to blow my entire life savings to buy a bunch of things that I'd never even heard of before but now "needed."

One of the first things that I "needed" to do was "baby-proof" the house. This is a smart idea for all parents—not only morons like me who buy bachelor pads with lots of stairs and decks and then decide to raise a child in them. I actually had a baby-proofing company come to my home to give me an estimate. The man who showed up told me that I should move. Cute.

The baby-proofing company either saw me coming or I lived in the world's most dangerous house. Aside from the stuff I could think of on my own, like putting a shield in front of the fireplace and locks on the cabinets, these guys bled me dry. When they were finished putting gates in front of the stairs and latches on closet doors they handed me a bill for 823 dollars! I said, "I asked you to baby-proof my house, not put up new fucking siding!"

The man calmly walked me out onto one of my decks and said, "You have four decks. All of them are pretty large. You needed three hundred and forty square feet of Plexiglas."

Now, believe me when I tell you I don't want my kid to fall from a deck, but 340 square feet of Plexiglas? Let me put that in perspective for you. That is precisely 110 feet more Plexiglas than Joan Rivers has in her face. My house looks like the whale tank at Sea World now. I wondered if I could just as easily have soldered all the doors to the patio and decks and saved myself a couple of hundred bucks. I obviously couldn't do that, though, and my home now has the most beautiful and expansive collection of Plexiglas panels imaginable. One afternoon, after a particularly violent storm had passed, I walked out onto one of my decks and saw that three of the panels had been blown out and disappeared. Not wanting to be bludgeoned again by the baby-proofing company, I looked out between the rungs of the railing on the deck and down at the land below. I thought to myself, It's only a couple hundred feet. There is plenty of grass and shrubbery down there, and don't babies bounce? To their credit, the baby-proofers came back to my house and replaced the missing Plexiglas panels for "free." When the highway robbers reemerged in my home, the guy handed me a tiny container and said, "I'm doing the Plexiglas for free because last time we were here I forgot to give you this and I could lose my job because of it."

"Oh, that's great. What is it?" I asked.

"It's called ipecac. One drop and anyone will immediately vomit."

Wow. Was this guy nuts? You don't give a comic a vial of instant puke! I immediately searched my brain for the perfect victim. Who had crossed me and how would I distract them away from their Diet Pepsi long enough to spike it with some good old-fashioned ipecac? Maybe I could invite one of my enemies over to bury the hatchet? The bottle of ipecac still sits in the cupboard in my kitchen and I lie in wait for someone to come over and piss me off.

Once the house has been baby-proofed, the next order of business is to fill our Plexiglas cages with the many new things to buy for a baby, things we have never shopped for before—bouncy swings, rocking chairs, pacifiers, plastic bathtubs, mobiles, strollers, diaper genies, sleep sacks, changing tables, gliders, blankets, and footies, to name a few.

That's right, there's more than that. You will also need an SUV or a minivan to haul all this shit home from the store.

If I ever decide to open a business later on in life, I will open a store that sells only baby furniture and retire to the Caribbean after two years with billions. Cribs, daybeds, and baby-changing stations are more expensive and more valuable to a new parent than all the diamonds in South Africa.

Shortly before Jackie was born, I went shopping for all the furnishings of my soon-to-be-son's nursery. Strict adherents to many religions will not buy baby products or open any baby shower gifts until after the child is born. They consider this an act of arrogance against God's impending gift. But I decided to go shopping because I didn't want my kid to be sleeping on the dining room table.

I went to a classy baby furniture boutique on Ventura Boulevard in Sherman Oaks. I shopped for less than one hour. I left with three pieces of furniture and all of their accessories and was quickly and pleasantly charged . . . seven thousand dollars.

Seven grand! What the hell just happened?! All I wanted was a freaking crib, and I wound up having to book an extra couple of gigs just to pay for it! I thought I was merely buying a crib. When I picked out the crib I wanted, the saleslady asked, "Do you have bumpers?"

No, I didn't have bumpers. Not only did I not have bumpers, I didn't even know what they were. Up until that moment, the only time I had heard the word *bumpers* used in a sentence was in reference to bumper cars, bowling alley bumpers, or the rear bumper that some jerk dented while I was in traffic on the 405. My house wasn't nearly large enough for a bowling alley or bumper cars, so I was forced to do what all men hate to do in the presence of a woman. I had to ask, "Wha?"

A bumper, it turns out, is the padded pillow that runs along the side of your baby's crib so his arm doesn't fall between the bars and snap off. Common sense would dictate that bumpers be sold with the actual crib, but I guess when it comes to baby supplies, common sense be damned.

I needed bumpers, so I bought bumpers. It turned out that I "needed" a lot of things that day, and I bought one of each of them. I "needed" a humidifier for a perfectly moist nursery, so I bought a humidifier. I "needed" a rocking chair to sit in while feeding the baby, so I bought a rocking chair to sit in while feeding the baby. I "needed" a daybed in case we wanted to sleep in the nursery with the baby, so I bought a daybed, which "needed" a trundle to accompany it.

Wait a second. What the hell is a trundle? A trundle is the bottom part of a daybed that slides out in case two people need to sleep in the baby's nursery. Gotcha. Trundle, check.

Shopping for my baby was like dealing with the mob. Every time I thought I was finished buying what I came in for, something else was "suggested" to me. Trust me, you don't want to be perceived as a cheapskate when it comes to your baby's nursery, so you wind up buying half the store. Jackie is too big for his crib now, but for three grand he had better crawl out of it the morning he wakes up to leave for college.

Aside from digging a giant, thirty-five-thousand-dollar hole for all of my kid's living expenses before he was even born, I found that shopping for baby-related items has an enormous upside: women LOVE would-be fathers. If you think a wedding ring makes you more attractive to the opposite sex, try shopping for baby food and diapers. Holy smokes! It seems that the moment you enter into this phase of consumerism, women rappel from the ceiling to offer help.

My theory on this subject is that women find commitment alluring. A woman may be arguing with her boyfriend about when they will get married and why can't he take out the trash and in you walk with an arm full of formula and a basket filled with Huggies number two, and the woman immediately makes a couple of assumptions that may or may not be true:

1. He is responsible! Ha. If they only knew how many times I forgot to put a dirty diaper in the *outside* trash cans and then watched in horror as my dog took five days to fully shit it out.

2. He is committed! Well, I *should be* committed . . .

But the moment I begin shopping for baby stuff, the chicks come out of the woodwork. They always lean just a little too close to tell you something, and they brush up against you as they talk. Thanks a lot, ladies. I was single for twenty-five years and had to buy enough booze for a generation of pirates. Where the hell were you then?

Here are some of the more baffling—and often disturbing— items on the baby shopping list.

BREAST PUMP

The most bizarre purchase I made due to impending fatherhood was a breast pump. Simply put, the breast pump is a medieval torture device that forcibly sucks milk from a woman's nipples and drops what it extracts into tiny plastic bags to be refrigerated and used as food later. Even though my friends tell me it tastes like half-and-half, its technical name is "expressed milk."

Every woman who has ever had to use a breast pump has my deepest sympathy. These contraptions look like something the Nazis designed to make couples never want to see each other naked again. It's truly humiliating for a woman to be hooked up to one of these things. The nipples get pulled a good four inches from the breasts and then sucked dry. I can imagine it hurts like a bitch—maybe even as extreme as a swift kick in the nuts.

Also, the sound the breast pump makes is a frightening series of slurps and whooshes accompanied by the constant droning of the breast pump engine, which never seems to tire of its torture. It's safe to say that if men ever had to be subjected to the breast pump, babies around the world would be fed strictly formula for their entire lives. Either that, or beer. Maybe Gatorade.

DIAPERS

The rule of thumb when shopping for baby products is that if it takes more than five minutes to figure out what it is or how it might be used, then you don't need it. The one exception to this rule is diapers. Just having the word *diapers* on your list is an adjustment to your psyche. What was once a trip for chips, beer, and turkey patties is now a trip for formula, baby diapers, and A&D ointment. And though diapers are a very tricky purchase, you definitely need them.

Buying diapers isn't like buying a can of soup or finding the deodorant that oozes from little holes. The margin of error is smaller than with other products. If you come home with the wrong olive oil, for example, you will probably hear something like "Oh, this isn't the extra-virgin I usually use, but I'll make do."

Not with diapers. If you come home with the wrong type of diapers, I assure you that you will immediately be dispatched to the supermarket to correct the damage. Who knew the world of diapers was so vast and expansive? I sure didn't.

Once Jackie was home, I was promptly sent out for diapers, so off I went. Little did I know that there are as many different types of diapers as there are babies. The first time I went to buy diapers, I was sweating as I perused the diaper section. I realized that I didn't even know what they came in. Do they sell diapers in a jar? Do diapers come bound up like firewood? Are they in the frozen department? Who knows? They're in an aisle that I've likely never even walked through before! And this is one of the astonishing things—there is an entire diaper aisle! Not a row or a shelf. Aisle three is *all* diapers! There are way too many choices! Huggies number one, Huggies number two, Huggies overnights, and of course, Huggies with wings (in case your kid is gay).

A few times I came home with the wrong diapers because I thought the baby on the package had to match the baby I had at home, like Garanimals. I would walk back and forth and mutter, "All these kids are Asian or black. Aren't there any white baby diapers?"

What I know now is that every baby is a different size and shape, and the diaper companies put out every conceivable size and shape of diaper to accommodate them. I once saw a bag of diapers that read "Holds up to fifty pounds." Holy mother of God! If your son goes to the bathroom and unloads fifty pounds, he doesn't need a diaper, he needs a job. Maybe some manual labor down at the docks is more suitable for your monster-dump baby! Do you have a high school senior at home walking around in Huggies twenty-twos? Do society a favor and potty-train that guy. No one wants the star quarterback in high school to have a full diaper in the huddle.

The bigger the baby, the higher the corresponding diaper number for his bottom. Jackie wore diapers until he was three.

Huggies number six. I was concerned about this because they don't make anything higher than six. What was my next choice if I didn't get him potty-trained in time? Adult diapers? Hefty bags?

Adult diapers are mixed in with the baby diapers at most supermarkets. What I find interesting is how many times I have stopped and stared at them and thought in all sincerity, It's not a bad idea.

We have all been stuck in rush hour traffic on the way to work after having that extra cup of coffee and bran muffin. Halfway through your commute your belly starts rumbling and you get the dump sweats. Forget the bus, exit-only, or carpool lanes, there should be an "I'm about to shit my pants!" lane. No one would have road rage anymore. Instead we would have road compassion. If you got cut off by some lady wedging her way into the "I'm about to shit my pants!" lane, you would think to yourself, Aww, poor gal, let me let her in. Those are cloth seats.

I have personally driven from Los Angeles to Las Vegas at least one hundred times. About 15 percent of that time, I have been stuck in bumper-to-bumper traffic in the desert thinking that I should have worn a diaper.

What is hilarious is that the more you have to take a dump on the way to work, the lower your standards drop as to where you would crap. You're switching lanes like a maniac with dump sweat running into your eyes and you're thinking, Oh good, miniature golf. Let me get over and I'll drop a deuce in the windmill. No one will ever know.

With adult diapers, we'd all drive to work carefree. We'd all behave like our children and let loose in our diapers. Hopefully, our parents would be at work waiting to change and powder us. Either them or an understanding colleague.

Nik and I have had long discussions about how bizarre being a child must be. One night we got punch drunk and kept laughing at why kids are so averse to potty training. They want to be like grown-ups in every single aspect of life with the sole exception of peeing in a bathroom, on an actual toilet bowl. Kids try to dress like us. Kids try to speak like us. Kids copy our mannerisms while talking on the phone. From a very young age, kids want to be exactly like us—except for the pissing and shitting part. Pissing and shitting in their pants is a behavior that a lot of children have an amazingly difficult time putting away.

Nik once said, "Is it because it feels good to shit in their pants? It can't feel good to stand there in your own piss. Don't get me wrong, it would be incredibly convenient to not have to pull the car over or leave a Broadway show or work meeting just to pee."

And she was right. We continued talking about the merits of *everyone* wearing diapers. We made a huge list of things that would run more smoothly if grown-ups were wearing diapers. Factories could double their output if employees could just stay seated at their stations and pee in a pair of adult Huggies. College students would never have to leave lecture halls. All car trips would have an immediate fifteen minutes shaved off their arrival time. And sleep! Imagine how much more sleep we would all get if we wore diapers under our pajamas! We would sleep ten hours straight and go to work completely invigorated.

At some point during this diaper discussion, my bride asked me if I had ever actually worn an adult diaper. I told her I hadn't and she told me she hadn't, either. Big surprise on both counts, right? But still, we both knew at that exact moment what had to happen next. We had to immediately go to the grocery store, buy adult diapers, race home, and try them on.

Well, when you are new parents, this becomes a fun night. Between the giggling on the way to the store and the giggling in the store and the giggling at the checkout counter, we no doubt looked like Cheech and Chong. When we got home, we tore into the diaper package like kids on Christmas morning. We wedged our bodies into our new toys. Just the act of putting your legs through the holes of an adult diaper is a very strange sensation. We then put our regular clothing on top of our diapers. We were now laughing like two people who had graduated from marijuana to mushrooms. We decided that if anyone in the world saw us at this moment, we would be committed to Bellevue. Once in Bellevue, we would think about the reason for being committed and laughing about it all over again would ensure that we would subsequently never be released. We then laughed some more, realizing that at Bellevue, we would no longer be the only adults in diapers. The laughter continued. So, we are finally in our regular clothes wearing our secrets underneath. Now it was just a waiting game. In hindsight, we should have drank a lot of water before we left for the store. Neither one of us had to pee right away, so we just walked around the house, giggling.

Eventually, I said to Nik, "The funniest part about this is that we are hysterically laughing and it is only a joke for two people."

She walked toward me and replied, "No, the funniest part about all of this is that you . . . don't . . . know . . . that . . . I . . . am . . . peeing . . . right . . . now!"

She was right.

The laughing and giggling reached dangerous levels. I was laughing the kind of laughs where you have to walk out of the room and concentrate on not laughing because you feel like if you keep laughing, you will die.

Suddenly I was jealous. Nik had experienced the sublime pleasure of pissing in a diaper and I had not. I stood still and leaned against one of the walls of the house, trying to will out a stream. When I finally was able to pee, it was euphoric. No wonder Jackie didn't want to be potty-trained! Peeing in a diaper is freaking awesome! To my surprise, it wasn't wet and disgusting like I had anticipated. The adult diapers were impressively absorbent and whatever came out of me magically vanished.

I'll be honest with you (hell, we've gone this far)—I could easily wear an adult diaper every day. I want to wear one on airplanes and I want to wear one every time I drive to Vegas. I could make it to Vegas in two hours if I didn't have to pull over to urinate. In all seriousness, Nik and I learned a very valuable lesson that night. We learned what it was like to be three years old. We learned that Jackie was hesitant to come out of his diapers because they were incredibly convenient. With our stupid, laughter-filled adult diaper night, we were better able to understand our child. I am not suggesting you go out and wear a diaper to get to know your kid better. However, I do suggest that you wear a diaper to know how great it feels to piss in your car. I also suggest that if you *do* go out and pee in an adult diaper for fun, don't tell anybody about it. I just told you and now you think I'm a freak.

Incidentally, I meet a lot of men who like to brag about never having had to change a diaper. I'm not one of them. I don't get grossed out by poop and I don't see wiping my kid's ass as some terrible job. In fact, I feel bad for those guys. Many of my most tender and private moments with Jackie have taken place while I was powdering his bottom. I have learned a lot about myself and my son while changing his diaper.

For starters, he seems to get an erection whenever I spray powder on his privates. I was confused when this first happened because I didn't think erections were something that happened until later in life. I was wrong. At three years old, my kid gets wood every once in a while and I try not to make a big deal out of it. The problem (or not) is that my kid is hung like a mule. I know I should keep everything cool and calm and act like it's completely normal, because after all, it is. I also know that when I first saw his erection, I should not have yelled, "Holy moly! Jesus, my man, have you got a rod on you!" This reaction was followed by a few days of "Daddy, what does *rod* mean?"

BABY (AND NANNY) MONITORS

I find it strange to think of a time when parents didn't use baby monitors. These days we all use them and even take them for granted. Back when you and I were kids, our parents laid us down in a room and closed the door. Then our folks would go about their business and simply assume that the baby in the room was fine. Even if we weren't. We could be upstairs in a crib, crying our eyes out with an overflowing diaper. Without the use of any monitors, our parents were oblivious to it all. As we freaked out, they were downstairs, playing cards with the neighbors. They had no idea that while they were sitting on a straight flush, we were accruing emotional scars for life. This is unheard-of and downright unsafe these days. I personally cannot imagine not using a baby monitor.

The monitors are incredibly low-tech little gadgets and very inexpensive, compared to how important they are. You can pick them up pretty much anywhere, and unlike every other piece of electronic equipment in my home, these are so easy that I can even set them up. The basic baby monitor looks like a walkie-talkie. It is the same size as a walkie-talkie, too. Hell, it's basically a one-sided walkie-talkie. You plug one of the monitors into the wall in the baby's room and then plug the other monitor into the wall in your bedroom. That's it. Simple. The difficult stuff happens after you have plugged the monitors in and have decided to settle down to sleep for the night. When you bought your baby monitors you did so with the express purpose of being able to hear your daughter if she should need you in the night.

Your baby might begin to cry because she is wet or your baby might call out because she is hungry. What no parent is ever prepared for is that not only do you hear your baby cry out but you are also treated to sounds you never knew your baby could make. Some nights in my house it sounded like Jackie had set up a goddamn petting zoo in his nursery. I would be woken up by the sounds coming from the monitor. The sounds weren't the usual wailing or sobbing or squealing a normal baby does. No. What I heard through that baby monitor was a pig snorting and a horse rooting around. I heard chickens clucking and I heard a cow mooing and chewing cud. Naturally, I was alarmed to hear these sounds, so I would run into his bedroom only to find him sleeping peacefully under his tiny blankets. On my way out I would check the carpet for hoofprints or hay. This is truly one of the more bizarre experiences in parenthood. Night after night, Jackie would make these barnyard sounds through the monitor, yet every time I went into his room he was as quiet as a mouse pissing on cotton.

Some nights, though, Jackie would make regular sleeping sounds. I would hear him shift his weight in his crib or sigh deeply. Those sounds are still fresh in my ears and forever in my heart. Some nights the monitor would, without warning, squelch static at an incredibly high decibel level, making our ears bleed. Luckily, there are volume knobs on the monitors and this is when they come in handy. You can turn the volume on a baby monitor all the way down to zero and there are still red dotted lights on the monitor that will jump up if there is sound coming from the baby. So, with the sound off, you can intermittently look up across the room to see if the monitor is redlining or if everything is mellow. Without the use of a baby monitor I would never have known that when Jackie turns his body completely around in his crib he sounds like a wild boar running through the woods. Much more important, without a baby monitor, my son would be alone in his nursery for four hours every morning while I slept like a baby myself. With a monitor on your nightstand, a child calling out "Daddy!" sounds as if he is on your pillow. It works out very well. The least you can do as a parent is wake up when your child does. (Unless, of course, you want to sleep late. Then just unplug the baby monitor and put it in a drawer for the night. When you walk into the nursery at noon, just act like everything is completely normal. This is a *huge* benefit of kids' not knowing how to tell time.)

A baby monitor's silence can also scare the shit out of you. You will be lying in bed reading and realize that your child has not made a sound in hours. You put your book down and listen very carefully for any sounds of life coming from the baby's room. After you take in a few minutes of absolute silence you rush into the nursery. At this point you are absolutely certain that something horrible has happened to your child. But, time after time, you walk nervously into the nursery and you see a baby lying in a crib, sound asleep. That baby does not have a single care in the world. This is his world—a room with a bed and a blanket and a parent who desperately wants to make sure he is safe.

You may also want to pick up a few nanny cams for the house. This seems like something you should buy at a spy shop, and let me tell you, they are incredible. You get a camera that is stuffed inside some teddy bear's belly and you can watch when the nanny is in your kid's room. You can also put them throughout the house and see who the fuck has been eating your Chips Ahoy. An odd phenomenon of a nanny cam is that when your baby is taking a nap, you find yourself in your bedroom watching the baby sleep on the nanny cam channel. You should be sleeping yourself but you can't. You are completely transfixed by the baby sleeping in the next room. She looks so beautiful and peaceful lying there. You study all of her motions and watch as she sucks on her bottom lip as she sleeps. Then you realize that if you walk fifteen feet, you can actually watch the baby sleep in person.

Parents are weirdos. All we have to do is walk in the nursery and watch perfection personified sleep. Instead we lie in our own beds, wide awake, watching the nanny channel.

One of the most horrible jobs a parent has when a baby is on the way is naming it. This will seem like an easy and fun task when you first get started but as the months drag on you will feel the pressure increase around you. Whatever name you choose for your baby is a name he will have to live with for the rest of his life. You should also make peace with the fact that no matter what name you choose, your child will most likely hate it their entire lives. (Do you like yours?)

The process of choosing a name for a person who does not yet have a personality seems arbitrary but is serious business. With rare exceptions, we really do grow into our names. If you name your daughter Porsche or Paris, she will most likely blossom into a gifted stripper. With girls you pretty much want to stay away from a name that is a vehicle or a snobby city. This includes names like Honda, Kawasaki, Tokyo, and Istanbul. No good can come from these names. Few people with these names will become positive members of society. Rarely, if ever, has anyone ever heard "Escalade, your witness." Or, "Is Doctor Lexus Mohr here?" Try to keep it as mainstream as possible when naming the little ladies. Don't get too hippy-dippy with your girl's name, either. If your daughter's name is Luna, that is an awesome name for a baby and a less awesome name for an actual person. At around the age of twelve, Luna is going to start focusing only on her chi and live her adult life teaching tantric sex and giving colonics.

Boy names are tricky but not as hard as girl names. Any boy name that you think sounds bad *is* bad. Not to defend Adolf Hitler, but his parents had to know that by naming their baby boy "Adolf" he would wind up one of the most evil men to walk the earth. Sure, as a baby, "Adolf" probably sounded cute as he slept in his crib in his footsies and little mustache. But as I said earlier, we grow into our names. Look around your kid's preschool class. Do you see any "Idi"s? Ever bump into a Genghis out on the playground? No, of course not. Those names were so horrible that only two sets of parents made the mistake of customizing their children's names for genocide. Obviously, every once in a while a Jim or a Jeffrey will slip through the cracks. There is no absolute formula for giving your child a name that will keep him from murdering and eating people.

The growing-into-our-names routine isn't only for bad people with bad names. Good people are born and named and they too grow into their names. Fred Rogers is the name of a baby who could only grow up to bring people joy. Shel Silverstein was never going to hurt anyone. The moment his folks named him Shel, the world was a safer place. If they had named him Saddam Silverstein, then maybe we would have had some serious problems. John Wooden is a name made for kindness and compassion. So is Vin Scully. These are gentle names for gentle men. Nik and I have to be extra careful. My last name is Mohr and her last name is Cox. Put our names together and say them out loud. Not good. Our poor kids are doomed no matter what we name them. It could be worse, I suppose. My last name could be Less. Seriously, what's worse for a kid, Mohr-Cox or Less-Cox? I have no idea; I just know to stay away from the car names for girls and the madmen names for boys. However, I have to admit, Idi is starting to grow on me. Idi Cox Mohr. Nice.

The bottom line is that nothing prepares any of us for parenthood. We are all completely unprepared and useless when faced with the drama, the sadness, the meltdowns, the disappointments. Fortunately, it all gets canceled out by the majesty, the laughter, the love, the magic. We are all equally unprepared when these wonderful moments happen. It is impossible to explain to a childless person what parenthood is like. You didn't know what love was until that baby was born. You find yourself answering "How is your son?" questions with quick, short answers like "He's good, thanks" or "Fine." You don't have enough time to tell that person that you know what God looks like because He sleeps in a bassinet next to your bed. To become a parent is to become awakened. Usually at five o'clock in the morning.

3

....

PROPER BOSTONIANS

When I was about seven, my family had a friend of my sister's from the neighborhood and her cousin from Florida over to our house for a turkey dinner. At one point during dinner, the cousin asked my sister, Julie, "Can I have some more tuhkey?" Julie asked her to repeat herself. Again the girl said, "Can I have some more tuhkey?" Julie then tried to make a joke and asked the girl, "Do you have a speech impediment or is that the way they talk down there?" Sadly, the girl hung her head and quietly said, "speech impedemet." It was pretty awkward and uncomfortable. After dinner, my sisters and I all fell on the floor laughing at "turkey."

I know we acted like complete jerks but kids are good at that. The reason I bring up this story is that it makes me think of how damn much I miss all of my son's little kid speech impediments. I'm not referring to phrases like "goo-goo, ga-ga" or "ma-ma, da-da." I am talking about the little ways that kids mispronounce words when they are three and four and five years old. Eventually they stop speaking this way and as you are sitting in rush hour traffic, you are overwhelmed by how much you miss your kid saying "bunket" instead of "blanket."

Another reason why it's so important not to miss a single day.

When Jackson and Nik first met, Jackie was just two years old and I was staying in a hotel for a couple of weeks. No one has a manual for how to care for a baby; it's very hard but it's even worse when you have to go it alone. I was lucky. I didn't have to go it alone for very long. Nik and I met on the set of the television show *Las Vegas*, which she was starring in. We hit it off instantly and immediately became inseparable. I told her about Jackson and she was excited to meet him. She agreed to come over and say hi. When I got back to the hotel that night, I got Jackie dressed, fed him some Froot Loops, and waited for my dream woman to show up. Nik knocked on the door, we kissed hello, and then I turned to Jackie and said, "C'mere, pal, I want you to meet a very good friend of mine."

Jackie waddled over and looked up at her without saying hello. After a few seconds, he pointed to Nik and asked, "That's a pretty girl?" Except at almost three it came out, "Dat's a peey guhl?"

I confirmed to him, "Yes, sweet boy, that is definitely a pretty girl."

Nik got down on the ground with Jackie and handed him a Matchbox car she had brought.

Jackie then asked her, "Ah you *my* peey guhl?"

Nik said, "Would you like me to be your pretty girl?"

Jackie quickly said, "Yes!"

Nik rubbed his head and said, "Then I am *your* pretty girl."

Jackie beamed the biggest smile I had ever seen on him and grabbed his future stepmom's hand and said, "Come peey guhl." He then led her down the hotel hallway to show her the place he thought was best to play Matchbox cars with a new peey guhl.

That was it. That thirty-second exchange morphed my stressful, suitcase, piecemeal life into heaven on earth.

We had a "peey guhl" now!

From that day forward, Jackie only called Nik "peey guhl." It was adorable. Nowadays he will let slip the occasional "Momma" or "Momma Nik" but she was pretty much "Peey guhl" from that day forward. Until he turned five years old.

After five, many of Jackie's adorable speech impediments quickly began to slip away forever. I was not prepared for this. I found myself saying certain words wrong just to prolong his baby talk. I realized that the loss of his speech impediments would symbolize the loss of his babyhood. Jackie was turning into a big kid and I missed the baby kid. I missed diapers. I missed long naps. I missed bottles in bed ("babas"). And I really missed walking around with him on my shoulders. Damn, I miss that.

Jackie carried a couple of speech impediments into his seventh year but eventually they vanished, too. He used to call the piano a "copiano." He said "kinvented" instead of "invented." "Vivel" instead of "bible." One day I told him he was saying the word *bible* wrong. Jackie told me that I was wrong. I reasoned with him that there was a pretty good chance that I was right.

I took the Bible off our shelf and showed him the letter *B*. "Look," I said. "B. Bible."

He didn't care. He said, "I'm gonna keep calling it Vivel. That's how I want to say it."

Fine with me. I wish I could have all of his weirdo speech impediments back for a day. I would love to hear him explain how he watched Peey guhl play the copiano. The little square blankets he rubbed as he fell asleep were called "dilkies" instead of silkies. I miss that!

I miss Jackson telling me, as he lay in his crib, "Two babas, two dilkies, match baseball." This means, of course, "Two bottles, two silkies, and watch baseball."

That was our routine every night. Jackie would drink a bottle in his crib as he tried to fall asleep. He would finish the bottle before he fell asleep so he would hold the empty bottle over his head and shout, "Mo ba ba!" Then, "Mo ba ba pees! Peey guhl, mo ba ba pees." It was like living with a drunken hobo. You couldn't really understand him and he was often belligerent. But I miss it. When kids turn from three to four, they lose a bunch of speech impediments. Fortunately, they can't shake how hard proper speech is and our four-year-olds still sound like drunks from Boston when they talk. If someone parallel parks in front of your house your son will yell out, "Dat cah just pahked ovah theya!" You will ask what he is talking about and he will descend further into the streets of Southie. "The guy got in his cah. He stahted it. Then he packed it ovah deya!" You'll ask, "Which car?" Your kid will yell back, "Dat cah! The dock cah ovah theya by the back daw!" Then like a proper Bostonian, kids will begin to scream the same sentence if they say it more than twice. *"Dat dock cah was pahcked ovah deya befoa!"*

I brought this point up to Nik and she said, "Kids also often shit themselves, like guys from Southie."

My peey guhl.

Whenever we would be out on walks and Jackie would mispronounce something, Nik would always tell me, "Remember it." She would also say, "One day he'll be speaking perfect English and you are going to miss this." Boy, was she right.

I miss Jackie saying "crown" instead of "crayon." This seems to be a very popular speech mishap among America's children. Kids love to draw with their crowns. They want to know where their crowns are and they want to know if you want to draw with crowns, too. I think the fine folks at Crayola should come up with an age-four-and-under crayon box called "Crowns." That would be sweet. The colors in the crown box would be lellow and bwown and gween and wed and bwack. That way after Jackie had dropped the speech impediment I would still have the crown box to remember the good times.

When kids are young, they can get away with being wrong, too. When a three-year-old says an incorrect answer, he can sneak by. Even the most evil of adults will have a hard time correcting a tiny-guy word mishap. The biggest douche uncle you have isn't going to say "It's pronounced 'railroad'! Not 'wail-woad,' you moron." And for the sake of your child's development, this is a good thing.

It took me a while to realize that I should just let Jackson confidently say the wrong thing when he felt like it. The important lesson for me was that I want my kid to feel confident enough to speak up. We also have to have faith that they will eventually right the linguistic ship in their little skulls and start saying things the right way. I used to correct Jackson constantly. Knowing his personality now, it is such a blessing that I stopped dropping the hammer on him. The last thing a kid needs is a fear of being corrected every time he opens his mouth.

One day, when Jackie was three, he and I were playing with Matchbox cars on the floor. He lined up all of his cars (about a hundred) across the living room floor. Sometimes I would be sneaky and turn one of the cars around on him. While looking at over a hundred cars spread out over about a hundred square feet he would immediately spot the backward car and rearrange it the way he wanted it. Whenever he had his cars out, he always had the same playing position. He would lie on his side with the bottom arm under his cheek and his hand stretched up out over his head. The free hand would take each car and run it back and forth and then he would set it back in line and move on to the next car. For some reason this drove me nuts. I wanted to play with the cars together. The problem was that Jackson had set up a very delicate and intricate game for himself. A game where if I were to touch anything, I would ruin it. I tried to talk him into playing with his cars differently. I showed him that he could set aside just one or two cars for flinging across the kitchen floor. He wasn't into it. So I decided to just watch some TV while my little Rain Man made his perfect rows of cars.

After a few minutes, Jackie came up to me on the couch and said, "Daddy, do you like this lellow car?"

"I think you mean YELLOW. That car is yellow."

Jackie looked blankly at me and spurted out, "That's what I said. Lellow."

For the next ten minutes I walked my kid through some half-assed diction lesson. I kept saying, "Listen to the difference. YELLow. LELLow. LELLow is wrong, YELLow is right."

Finally Jackie said, "Can I have my car back?"

I gave him his car and noticed that instead of putting it back into his perfect rows, he went to the kitchen and put it in the garbage. When he turned to come back into the room he had tears in his eyes and his bottom lip was shaking. I asked him why he threw out his YELLow car.

"I didn't frow it out, I'm just keeping it dare."

Then, Jackson went downstairs to his bedroom. In our house that is the equivalent of a major tantrum because Jackie so rarely has tantrums. I was so mad at myself for correcting him. So what if he got the word *yellow* wrong? Who really cares if he says "frow" instead of "throw"? I didn't have any fear that my kid was going to be in junior high yelling out "Hey! Frow me the football!" I should have just left him alone and let him speak like all little three-year-olds speak. I felt terrible. I got down on my knees in my living room and I prayed to God for what all parents need maybe more than anything. Patience. Then patience rang my doorbell.

Sometimes the best way to appreciate your kids is to watch someone else spend time with them. On this particular night, that is what happened to me. Mac was on his way over to meet Jackson for the first time. Nik's father and I have gotten along from the moment we met. When I picked Nik up for our first date he made it very clear to me that she was his little girl. He explained how once you are in the family circle, you are in, but once you screw up and leave, "there ain't no coming back."

Fair enough.

Anyway, on this particular evening, Mac was stopping by the house on his way home from work. I had become so frustrated during the last few hours by being a lousy father that I had completely forgotten about the visit. The doorbell rang, I looked up, and his sweet, smiling face was at my front door.

I went down to Jackie's bedroom to tell him he had company. He was lying on his bed, rolling a Matchbox car back and forth across the top of a pillow. I said, "Hey pal, Pretty Girl's daddy is here." He bolted up from the bed and started up the stairs. He was really excited to meet the man who "borned" his pretty girl. ("Borned" is another wonderful speech impediment that Jackie has long outgrown. Instead of saying someone is your mother or father, he would say that that person "borned" you. Nik and I always loved it and never corrected him on that one.)

Jackie was still holding his Matchbox car when he reached Mac. They said hello to each other and Mac quickly got down on his knees and asked to see the car. Jackie obliged and Mac said, "That is a '66 Corvette. I used to have one of those. That is a really, really neat car."

Jackie agreed. My boy then led his newest best friend to the living room, where over a hundred cars were still spread out everywhere. Mac's reaction was, "I like what you're doing here. The cars are set up in a very nice pattern."

Again Jackie agreed. For the next hour or so I watched a very gentle and tender relationship begin. They both borned it. Mac spoke to his grandson in a very relaxed tone of voice (his usual) and he also listened to every story Jackie had to tell as if he were receiving highly valuable information. Compared to the way I had behaved earlier, having Mac here now was like meeting Yoda. Sometimes we forget that when our kids are talking our ears off, they are doing it because what they are saying is important to them. Don't worry, I'm not going soft on you here. I fully realize that the reason we tune our kids' stories out is that they are so freaking boring! I swear that every single kid I have ever met who wasn't mine had way more interesting stuff to talk to me about. Have you ever noticed that? Other people's kids tell me stories and they have a subject and a predicate and usually they will even have a theme. Not our kids. Talking to your own kid is like talking to a coked-up drunk. Not much of the conversation makes any sense and eventually you realize that he is making it all up as he's going along. There should be a place where you go to swap a story or two with other people's kids.

As parents, we will be two blocks into the drive home from preschool and want to jam pencils in our ears because we can't tolerate how freaking boring our kids are. Everyone has always told me that kids say the darnedest things but my kid can be a total snore. And he'll not only be a snore, but he'll exaggerate just enough for me to get sucked into the conversation to let him know that I don't believe him. If my boy tells me a Pokémon story, I can tune it out. However, if he tells me a Pokémon story and happens to say that his friend has a Pokémon card where if you hold it you can fly, I have to say my piece. I will explain to him that if there were a card that if you held it you could fly, his friend would have been famous and on the news because no such card exists yet in the universe. Then he will say some other things that are exaggerated or just plain made up. Each time, I take the bait and let him suck me into talking about Pokémon in the car instead of the lack of Dodgers starting pitching because let's face it, that's what we should be talking about. There have been so many kid things that have become completely worthless but at the time we all collected them like fools. Cabbage Patch Kids come to mind. So do Beanie Babies and Webkinz. We pile up on these things because our kids convince us that they will be worth money some day. Ten years later they are useless. But in ten years every team in baseball will still be paying top dollar for starting pitching.

Did your son ever come home from school one day and out of nowhere have a friend whose word is the gospel? It is always a kid you have never heard of. Suddenly this mystery child is telling your naïve kid tall tales and convincing them that all the stupid shit they are making up is true. Very quickly after the first mention of this child, your son starts taking the word of the new kid over the word of you.

One day Jackie came home from preschool telling me things told to him by JAMES (he said the name James louder than the other words in the sentence, so I capitalized it).

"Daddy, when I was at JAMES's house, he told me there was an incredible flood."

"Oh, really?"

"Yup. JAMES told me that the flood was so bad that his

bedroom windows were underwater and water went all the way up to the chimney of the house."

I asked Jackie if he believed JAMES. He told me that he did. I then calmly explained that since James lived up on top of Mulholland Drive, if his house was underwater, the entire city would have been underwater and I would have probably remembered that event.

My kid wouldn't budge. He went on to say, "But it could have happened because JAMES said it happened."

This will go back and forth for a while until I realize that this James is a guy he really believes in. In the credibility department, somehow I have become second fiddle to this little Fonzy at school. One afternoon on the drive to Jackie's karate class he told me, "Daddy, JAMES has a rainbow belt. Isn't that so cool?"

I said that I was pretty positive that no such belt exists— that his buddy was exaggerating his story. Jackie didn't think the story was far-fetched at all. Even after I went through the colors of the belts with him, he still believed his friend had a rainbow belt. I asked him to tell me all the belt colors.

My son counted them off: "White, yellow, orange, purple, blue, green, green with a brown stripe, brown, brown with a black stripe, and then black."

I started to say something like "I rest my case" but he quickly jammed in "And JAMES's rainbow belt."

It was hopeless. There was no way I was going to be able to convince my kid that his new buddy lied to him. After dropping him off at karate, I sat for the next half hour during the lesson stewing over JAMES's stupid stories. Why couldn't Jackie understand that I would never lie to him about stupid stuff like fake floods and rainbow belts? As asinine as it sounds, this really bothered me. My son was taking the word of a five-year-old as the truth over the facts that his father was presenting. It made me nuts. Every time Jackie would bring up a bullshit James story I would tell him how it was impossible for it to be true. Each time, he insisted that I was wrong and James was right. It got to the point where one day I had to restrain myself from swearing in front of my child.

At one red light, Jackie began a story, "JAMES said . . ."

I almost spun around in my seat and said "Fuck James! James sucks!"

Instead at the last second I pulled up short and said, "Forget James. James isn't here!"

I have to pat myself on the back for that one.

Back to the lellow problem at hand. I had completely forgotten that what my son was telling me was very important to him. Each car that he had perfectly lined up was exactly as he wanted it. Who cares if he said "lellow" instead of "yellow"? The root of the matter was that my son was showing what was fascinating stuff to him and I was taking time out of his glory to correct his speech. He was not quite three yet and I was correcting him like a freaking schoolmarm.

Meanwhile, Mac asked Jackie, "How many cars do you have in your hand?"

Jackie would count them out: "One, five, two, eleventeen, lefty-one!"

Mac very calmly and simply said, "That's right."

Oh.

Then I realized that I am a complete asshole.

Jackie and his new grandfather had many such conversations that night. When asked what was one plus one, Jackie responded proudly, "One!" Mac, again, said, "You got it."

As the evening went on, Jackie opened up and really talked his face off to Mac. He explained things that I would have found completely ridiculous if I weren't watching a veritable rocket scientist nod his head at them. I prayed again later that night. I didn't ask for anything. I just gave thanks. I prayed for patience earlier and patience rang my doorbell. I watched my Jackson, the same guy who was driving me nuts—the same kid whom I drove nuts—with a new listener, and watched him blossom into a chatterbox. Mac never corrected Jackie that night and more importantly, I learned to correct him a lot less.

Incidentally, if you have a twelve-year-old at home who counts to eleventeen you might want to keep him back a year or two. But at three years old, embrace the silly things that your child says. One day Nik was getting ready to do a talk show. She went into the bedroom to put on a cocktail dress. When she was finished making herself up, she called her boys in to see if we liked what she was wearing. She looked stunning. Jackie slapped his forehead and said, "I can't take my mind!"

We loved it.

To this day we all say it like it is the Queen's English. If we see a cool special effect in a movie or if we see a homeless guy take a dump in the middle of the street we'll say, "I can't take my mind!"

One Halloween, Nik went to Western Costumes and rented the actual Mary Poppins outfit worn in the movie. Jackie had *Mary Poppins* in his DVD player and was really wearing it out. He knew the entire movie by heart. One night, while he was in the bathtub, my bride slipped into the Mary Poppins costume (complete with carpetbag) and walked into the bathroom. In a perfect, proper English accent, Nik sang to the boy, "A spoonful of sugar helps the medicine go down, the medicine go down, the medicine go down. In the most delightful way!"

Jackie's mouth was frozen wide-open. Finally, he whispered, "Oh. My. Moly."

We still use that one, too.

One afternoon while driving by the ocean, I was acting like a complete freak and Nik called me a goof. I continued to act like a freak and from the back of the car Jackie screamed, "You GOOP!" I don't think I have said the word *goof* since. I know your kid has a few doozies that you still use. At least I hope so.

Jackson took a long time to learn to talk. He was born two and a half months premature. I don't think his being born premature had anything to do with his slow speech but maybe I got you to think "aww" and I am cheap enough to take any response from you I can get. I have noticed, though, that whenever you tell someone your child was premature, they always have to outdo your preemie story. They instantly tell you how they know someone born earlier and how that person is now enormous. If, for example, I tell a guy at the park that my son was born two months premature, the man will automatically tell me, "My cousin was born five months premature and now he's six foot seven and weighs three hundred and forty pounds!" Okay, guy at the park. You win the premature baby story contest. Asshole. My son was born two months premature *and now he's six two in first grade and he can dunk!*

And he had a slow, slow journey into speech. At one point I had to bring him to a special speech teacher in the San Fernando Valley. The woman was named Beth—to torture the children with lisps—and she was fantastic. At the time Jackie had a hard time saying *e* sounds. Instead of saying "Merry Christmas," he said "Merra Christmas." "Berra" instead of "Berry" (and no, he didn't mean Yogi, much as I had hoped otherwise).

Every day I tried to get Jackie to spit that *e* out but to no avail. I told him to say what I said and he couldn't. I would have him just say the letter *e* and then try to get him to immediately stick it at the end of *Dad.* "Dad-eee."

"Jackie, say *eeeeee.*"

"Eeee."

Then I would say, "Jackie, say Da*deeee.*"

He would say, "Da*daaa*."

I was apparently a lousy teacher. Beth, on the other hand, was the kid whisperer. To this day I am still not quite sure how she got Jackson to speak properly. We walked into her office and she sat on the floor with him. That is something I was beginning to notice more and more. (If you want a kid's attention you have to get down on the ground. Again, it's like talking to drunks.) She then took a fake Oreo cookie out of a plastic cookie jar and told him, "I want you to put this cookie in the doggie's back." Jackie took the plastic Oreo out of Beth's hand and dropped it inside the plastic dog's back. Beth said, "Good!" She said it so loudly that I jumped a little. Then Beth took Jackie's hand and said, "I'll let you do it again if you say DaDEEE." He said "DaDa" and Beth pulled the cookie back toward her. Again, she told him to say "DaDEEE." He stared at her for a moment and when she started to hand the fake cookie out toward him he shouted, "DaDEEE!" Beth shouted back, "Good boy!" and handed Jackie the fake cookie, which he put inside the fake dog. This went on for a half hour with Beth pushing the envelope with different words and sounds. Each time he couldn't do it, she pulled the fake cookie back. Every time she pulled the fake cookie back my son would shout what she wanted him to. The simplicity was exceptional. Who knew that to be a great children's speech therapist all you need are plastic cookies and a piggy bank?

I know it wasn't the piggy bank or the fake plastic Oreo cookie. It was Beth and her energy that opened my son's mind.

61

To this day I am grateful, and Beth, if you happen to be reading this: Thank you. You are incredible.

After all the speech impediments are gone and your children are no longer speaking like drunks from South Boston, they will make up their own expressions. They may say something like "Oh my moly" or "I can't take my mind." Please don't correct them.

Every once in a while in the middle of all the misused phraseology and expressions, if they are feeling especially confident they will reach even further in their little brains and say something that blows you away. When Jackie was about five, he was telling Nik and me a story about something that happened to him at night. In the telling of the story he did not make it clear *which* night. We kept asking him, "Did this happen last night?" He would tell us, "No." We would ask him when and he would say he couldn't explain it. After he grew frustrated enough, he calmly leaned forward in his car seat and said, "Okay, let me explain it to you." Whenever a kid starts a sentence with "Let me explain it to you," a great story usually follows. We told him he didn't have to explain it to us. We just wanted him to tell us which night this story happened. His response was a slow and metered "The night that brought us today." Wow. It was like Yeats was in the backseat of my car. "The night that brought us today" by e. e. cummings. He did mean last night but to him "last night" meant no more nights. My son properly renamed all last nights, "The night that brought us today." Thanks again, Beth.

4

HOURS AND HOURS OF FUN

There are very few things that I do not like about children. One of the negatives about kids is that they are all morning people. I am not a morning person. I have never been a morning person. For fifteen years, I spent nights in hotel rooms on the road falling asleep as the sun came up, once I had finished watching every movie on the menu. I spent my entire twenties waking up at two in the afternoon and after being awake for three hours, taking a nice one-hour nap. Sleeping late is in a performer's blood. In show business, everything happens at night. Shows start at nine and then there is a second show at eleven-thirty. That means our job *starts* at nine. That translates into getting ready for work at 8 P.M. After a show you are incredibly jazzed up and the thought of sleep is ridiculous. It takes hours of drinking and talking with friends and hours on the computer to wind down from two comedy shows.

Suddenly, I live with a person who pops up in bed at six-thirty in the morning. Most kids never sleep past eight unless they have a concussion or something. What am I supposed to do with a child at six-thirty in the freaking morning? Everything is closed. Anything that opens before 9 A.M. is either an all-night Laundromat or a diner. How entertaining is it to my child to watch a spin cycle and eat sausage?

Why do kids all wake up so damn early? It's as if they are all preparing for the life of a longshore fisherman. I tried everything to get my son to sleep later. If I put him to bed after 9 P.M., he wakes up earlier for some reason. Through trial and error, I have learned that the earlier I put my son to sleep, the longer he sleeps in.

A few nights I tried putting him down at ten o'clock, only to have him spring awake at five. If I put my son to bed at eight, he will sleep until six-thirty. Where is the baby that sleeps until eleven? I want that one. I would even pay extra for him. How wonderful it would be to walk into a nursery at ten-thirty in the morning and have my baby boy roll over with one eye open and say "Hey, what time is it? There was a *Columbo* marathon on last night and I couldn't turn it off. The two-parter with Johnny Cash. Jesus, what time is it? Is there any coffee?"

These children, sadly, do not exist. If they did, school would start at noon and prime-time television would start at nine. Often you hear someone exclaim, "There just aren't enough hours in the day!" Whoever says this doesn't have kids. Every hour of the day as a parent gets slower and slower as the clock creeps toward bedtime. I will wake up with my son, make him breakfast, walk the dog, play with his cars, and go get gas in my truck. After all of these chores and activities have been accomplished, I will look at my watch and it will be 10 A.M. Okey-dokey, now what?

"Hey, I have a great idea!" I'll say, "Let's go to the park!"

Off we go to the park and between stifling yawns, I watch my son swing from monkey bars and play in the sand. My son doesn't understand why I won't let him use the slide (*It's still wet from the night before.* I never could understand why in a city like Los Angeles—where it hardly ever rains—everything is soaking wet every day) and I have to bribe him away from the slide with a game of soccer on the freshly sprinkled wet grass. By the time we are finished at the park, my son looks like a homeless person. His bottom is dark with water and his knees, elbows, and forehead are covered in dark, wet sand. After the park, I feel like I have been awake for an entire day already but as I look at my watch, I see that it is not even noon! Why are there so many hours in the day? I will make my son a peanut butter and jelly sandwich and some grapes (no, wiseass, I don't make the grapes) and we settle in for some cartoons. After an hour of

Thomas the Tank Engine or *Tweenies* or, God forbid, *Boohbah* (if you don't know what this show is, it makes the Teletubbies look like *Masterpiece Theater*), the clock mercifully says 1:00. Nap time! This is a big crossroads in each and every day we spend together. Mainly because I want desperately to nap and he doesn't want to nap at all.

After some serious negotiating, I sometimes will get my guy down for a nap. When he wakes up at around two-thirty in the afternoon I read to him and take him back to the park, which is hopefully dry by now. Dinner is at five and after dinner we walk the dog around the neighborhood and visit our friends on the street for some conversation (mostly about cars), and then take a bath. After all this is accomplished there is still about an hour before bedtime. This, my friends, is when time simply stops. Every night at this hour I find myself hearing and feeling every click of my watch's second hand even though I love being with my son and wouldn't trade a single moment of it for any other activity on earth.

The problem is, at seven-thirty at night I have done every single activity known to man. I have even been to the park twice. Reading my son a few more books knocks off only about thirty minutes. The television mocks me from its console in the corner of my living room. It seems to be saying "If you just turn me on you can leave him here for hours." But I think too many parents turn to TV to entertain their kids and I seem to be a much better parent with the television off. So the television stays off and the minutes and seconds sloooowly roll by. Finally, after a veritable eternity, I tell Jackie it is bedtime.

Each and every night, he protests. He acts as if the announcement of bedtime in his near future is some bombshell I just pulled out of my ass and it is *so* unfair of me to stop the party when it is really starting to get swinging. I make his bottle and get him his two silky blankets and walk with him down into his bedroom. I sing a little Chet Baker to him or maybe some U2. I lay him down in his crib and we say a prayer, thanking God for the wonderful day we just had, and as I walk out of his room, he will begin the masterful art that all children are born with. The art of stalling.

"Daddy, what is this?"

"What?"

Then he just looks blankly back at me as if to say "I don't know. You think of something. That is as far as I thought it."

After about ten minutes of mindless back-and-forth and answering questions like "What does *blanket* mean?" or "What does *bottle* mean?" I tell him I will be in the next room typing on my computer. It seems to be a great comfort to my boy to know where I am as he drifts off to sleep. To know that I am not leaving him. He just wants to know where I am.

If he only knew that after he falls asleep, I am the one with all the questions. I get up from my bed a half-dozen times during the night. I have to make sure he hasn't kicked off his blankets. I need to be sure the baby monitor is on and I can hear him if he wakes up in the middle of the night (he does, at 1 A.M., like clockwork). I wonder if I should have put socks on him and whether his feet will get cold while he sleeps.

When I was a child and probably when you were a child, too, the sound of a shouted "Go to sleep!" was pretty common. Not these days. Nope, we of the "I love you" dads' generation negotiate and explain. We hold and hug and kiss and love. We wake up early, to the tune of our kids' Cheerios. As I lie in my bed, knowing I will have to wake up in five hours, I think back to a time when I was single and had no children. I slept as late as I wanted. I drank and smoked pot. I took two-, sometimes three-hour naps. I never had to change a diaper filled with shit and wipe another human being's ass.

As I drift off to sleep I realize that I am living the best life imaginable.

5

. . . .

BABY VIRGINS

Does anyone reflect fondly on their first time? First times are terrible. They are messy and awkward and generally tend to leave us in an emotional state of disrepair. But we put so much stock in first times, especially as parents. We wait with bated breath for our baby's first steps and first words. And then a couple of months go by and we no longer really care that they are walking and talking. It actually becomes an enormous nuisance. You can't even run out and grab something from the car because your walking baby will stumble around the house and rediscover electricity or find your pot. When your body is racked with stomach flu and all you need is an hour of sleep, you don't think the sound of your baby's voice is very magical at all. In fact you would give everything you own for them to just be perfectly quiet for just one day. Don't get me wrong, I acknowledge that a baby's first steps are exciting, but if they are so important, shouldn't we celebrate walking longer? Wouldn't it be great if your seven-year-old walked in the door from school and you and a few of your friends filmed it and clapped and told him what a good boy he was?

When Jackie was two, I took him for his first haircut. Since that day I've always looked forward to his haircuts because I love the way he sits like a little gentleman as the barber trims his hair and explains to him that the clippers are going to tickle. I looked in the Yellow Pages and found a place, the Circus Ball on Ventura Boulevard, that specializes in children's haircuts. The owner of this place knows what the hell he is doing. Four video games are in one corner of the shop and next to the video games is one of those quarter eaters that have a claw and two levers that are supposed to dip down and retrieve treasures for your child. (Unless you have forty dollars in quarters, I suggest avoiding this machine altogether.) Bright balloons and rainbows are painted on the walls and children's songs play from the overhead speakers. A guy named "Eddie Spaghetti" cut Jackie's hair. I wasn't sure how long Jackie would sit still for an official haircut, so I told Mr. Spaghetti to give him just a quick trim. Eddie Spaghetti proceeded to take out handkerchiefs and coins and perform magic tricks for Jackie, who was not impressed. He looked blankly at Eddie Spaghetti as if to say "My dad makes stuff disappear all the time." He had every reason to be unimpressed. What is the logic behind making coins disappear from a three-year-old? When I make things disappear they are things of far greater importance. Things like drum kits and race cars regularly vanish into thin air in my house. Any toy that makes noise is bound for the vanishing act the day it arrives.

Eddie Spaghetti kept marveling at his own abilities and Jackie and I both began to grow restless. We came in for a couple of haircuts, not some two-bit magic act by a barber. Jackie sat through his haircut like a good boy and when he was finished the receptionist gave him a bright red lollipop. I sat in the chair next and I told the Magnificent Spaghetti that he didn't need to show me any tricks. After five minutes, my haircut was finished, too. I went to pay and the gal at the desk told me that Jackie's haircut was twenty bucks. I handed her forty, since we received two haircuts, and she held the money in her hand, palm to the ceiling, and stared at me. I asked her what was wrong and she told me I owed her another seven dollars. I said, "I thought you said the haircut was twenty dollars?"

She said, "Your son's haircut is twenty dollars. Yours is twenty-seven dollars. You owe me another seven."

How does that work? I get charged an extra seven bucks? Why, because I have a bigger head? Shouldn't I get a discount for bringing my kid to this place? Did they think that he brought me? Sure, my kid pored over the Yellow Pages and after half an hour, although he can't freakin' read, he decided to bring me here. Then he started up the Escalade and drove me here and told me to act like a good daddy along the way.

I didn't get any magic tricks, my head looks like a golf course, and I have to cough up an extra seven bucks. Good luck on repeat business. Next time I suggest you give the *adult* the seven dollars off. It would even out in the end pricewise but at least then I would be operating under the illusion of having gotten a break.

I tell you the story about my son's first haircut because it is a great example of "monumental firsts" that don't live up to our expectations. Nik and I waited until my son's hair was past his shoulders before we brought him in for his first haircut. We waited two good years. Some parents wait way too long to cut their kid's hair. You've seen them walking around the mall or down your street with their little long-haired freak. They get super offended when you guess the sex of the baby wrong. You say, "How old is she?" And the parents will snort back, "*He* is three and a half!" Then you should say "Then why don't you cut his fucking hair? Who are you raising? Captain Caveman?" The parent will walk off in a huff but who cares? They shouldn't be out at the movies with a three-foot Allman Brother. If I am at my son's soccer game and I can't read the number on the back of your kid's jersey because of his hair, then I am just calling him "her" the entire game and you have to live with that. It's your choice. There's a magician in the San Fernando Valley who would love to give your son a trim.

Parents tend to get it completely wrong when deciding what is important and monumental. Every time the preschool teacher sends my kid home with "artwork" we proudly hang it up on the refrigerator. The problem is that the teacher just keeps the artwork coming. Then the kindergarten teacher starts sending home "artwork." After kindergarten, the first-grade teacher starts sending home reams of "artwork." Eventually there is no room left on your fridge. Every square inch of your desk at work is covered. You have framed a dozen pieces of "art" and hung them on the walls of your house. You have given "artwork" to your parents to frame and hang. One day you realize that all of this artwork is terrible. You realize that the reason the teachers keep sending it home is that they can't stand the sight of it. The moment the paint or ink is dry on the paper, they stuff it into our kids' little backpacks and send it our way. Don't get me wrong, if you have a young Picasso at home or a budding Matisse, then by all means hang the artwork up in the house. If my son is doing Basquiat charcoal drawing in kindergarten, then by all means, I'll frame it. One thing that none of us needs anymore is hand turkeys at Thanksgiving. I'm good. We are all set on hand turkeys in this house for the next three lifetimes. If you are a teacher and you are reading this, please stop sending home hand turkeys. Also, just because my kid held a crayon and that crayon touched paper, that doesn't mean that it is a work of art. You keep it. It's my gift to you. You're welcome.

Another first that I can't say I recall fondly is Jackie's first "big-boy potty" foray. But maybe that's because it took nearly half a decade. However, I need to tell all parents reading this book that there is no proper timetable for potty training. Some kids are pooping in the toilet at two. Other kids don't get the hang of it until they are five. Obviously, if your son is fourteen and walking around in diapers, you might want to take him to see someone.

Not all kids take naturally to potty training. Some kids really hate it and find it terrifying. Of course, my son was one of these kids. He fought tooth and nail to stay away from the toilet bowl. I wasn't sure why. While I appreciate taking a leak in an adult diaper on the way to Vegas, I can't understand why any human being wouldn't jump at the chance to stop shitting in their pants. It can't feel good. You can't possibly be as good a dancer, either, but I digress.

It is absurd the lengths we go to make the simple act of taking a crap seem like the most fun our kids will ever have. Some parents drop little targets in the toilet to encourage their boys to pee on them. That isn't a terrible idea, I guess; but how do we extend that strategy to when the kid is going number two? Maybe you could put tiny maps of Hiroshima and Nagasaki in the toilet and tell your three-year-old that his asshole is the Enola Gay.

Once they hit four years old, I feel like whatever works is fine. I told Jackie that I would buy him toys if he pooped in the toilet. It didn't work.

As a concept, the "potty" is an interesting one. Essentially it is a tiny interim toilet for kids to sit on and practice craps. This mini-throne is usually brightly colored and shaped like a duck or a pony. This must be very hard on a three-year-old's psyche. The poor kid must be thinking, My parents give me a big round of applause every time I take a crap on this duck's neck. If your kid doesn't want to go to the bathroom in their mini-duck toilet or in the regular toilet, unfortunately there is nothing you can do but wait. I promise you that one day they will figure it out. I was pulling my hair out for a year when Jackson would recoil in horror at the sight of the toilet. His horror was in direct proportion to the horror I felt at the massive dumps he was leaving behind in his Huggies number six. Because he wasn't potty-trained when it came time for preschool, Nik had to actually find a preschool where the teachers would change diapers. It turned out to be one of the best preschools in California but I think the fact that their educators were willing to change loaded diapers put them way over the top.

Nik and I tried to get Jackie potty-trained for about a year. Nothing worked. I mean, nothing. I even offered him money! I would have him not wear diapers around the house and tell him to let me know when he felt like he had to go potty. He never felt like he had to go potty. In fact he would go all day without any urge at all and then the moment I put him in the bathtub, he would crap. No one ever really provided us with instructions for how to remove floating turds from a full bathtub. I guess if we had fish, we could always use that little aquarium net and scoop them out. But I don't have fish. I was livid at Jackson for doing such a disgusting thing. I immediately pulled him out of the bathtub by his armpits and held him up over the toilet and began to set him down on the seat.

What happened next is something I have seen done only in cartoons. Jackie lifted his legs up in the air so that I couldn't put his bottom on the seat. I know it sounds like no big deal but you have to understand that he was a skinny four-year-old. I needed his legs in order to sit him on the toilet seat. With his legs pulled up so his knees were over his head, whenever I tried to sit him on the toilet seat he just slipped down through it with his skinny butt almost touching the toilet water. No matter which way I twisted or turned, I couldn't jimmy my kid's ass so it flattened out onto the seat. He just kept lifting his legs like Bugs Bunny up and around his head so no piece of thigh would touch the seat. I eventually realized that he was also crying. I felt terrible. He was truly terrified. Up until this point, I thought he was just being obstinate. He wasn't. Jackson had a very real terror when it came to the toilet bowl. I didn't want to make potty-training any more stressful than it already was and yet here I was lowering a horrified four-year-old into toilet water. I was adding months onto potty training. I was blowing it.

My terrible feelings about this were equal in magnitude to my feelings of confusion as to why my kid was so damn afraid of the freakin' toilet bowl. I was retelling this story to Nik's father, Mac, and when I asked him, "Why the hell is he so scared of the toilet?" Mac calmly looked at me and with a been-there and done-that twinkle in his eye simply said, "It's a big hole."

6
....

KID LOGIC

One afternoon Jackie and I were walking through the promenade in Santa Monica to the bookstore, when I noticed a clown making balloon animals for tips. I stopped Jackie and pointed across the promenade. "Look, Jackie!" He turned his head. "Look! There is a clown over there!" Jackie tried to find the clown that I was pointing to (kids have the worst sense of direction) and after about thirty seconds, he spotted him and stared at the clown. Finally he looked up at me and said, "That's not a real clown, Daddy, that's just a guy dressed up as a clown."

Of course, he was right. But why did it stand out to me at the time as so odd? I forgot to mention that the man/clown was a bit destitute. In fact, if I were to be completely honest, I would say that the guy was a few balloon animals from being homeless.

Okay, if we're *really* being honest, the guy was a horrible, dirty, drunk, and shitty clown. Jackie was right. He had no business laying claim to the title of Clown. He was just some drunkard who got some greasepaint and baggy clothes and was willing to stand in the heat for two hours for a few bucks. This guy didn't even have the common decency to wear clown shoes. I looked at his feet and he was wearing L.A. Gear sneakers.

I guess what struck me were Jackson's words: "real clown." He had so completely dismissed the man as not being a "real clown." What exactly was a real clown? Was Jackie referring to all the baby clowns who are born each year to real clown parents in clown hospitals? I didn't think so, but when you spend enough time around a four-year-old you begin to question your own logic and sanity. I spent the rest of our walk to the bookstore imagining a real clown birth. I pictured the clown wife with her giant clown shoes up in the stirrups. I pictured all the clown doctors with their freaky clown hair and their big scary eyes above their masks. They probably would have to have a special clown mask to accommodate their enormous noses. I pictured real clown nurses squirting the mother in the face with a seltzer bottle and the baby with a full face of makeup shooting out of a clown vagina. (I will pause here and assume that you have never read the words *clown* and *vagina* in the same sentence. You're welcome.) The placenta would be a big pie and naturally it would shoot out of the clown vagina (you're welcome) and smash the doctor in the face. The real clown couple wanted it to be a surprise so they wait anxiously for the doctor to tell them what they had. Finally, the real clown doctor says, "Congratulations! It's a . . . *sad*-faced clown!" Then the real clown couple hug and cry because they already have three happy-face clowns and were really hoping for a sad-faced hobo clown baby.

Then I thought to myself, If it was a true clown birth, forty baby clowns should climb out of the clown vagina one after the other like they do with the little cars in the circus. Then I realized I had been pulling on a door that said push for a good three minutes.

As much as I wanted to laugh at what my kid had said, I couldn't shake the undeniable truth that he was right. The guy on the promenade was just a drunk literally masquerading as a clown.

Kid logic will make you rethink your entire education. One day Jackie and I were driving to the park and I was explaining to him that when he got older he could do whatever he wanted for a living. He told me he wasn't sure what he wanted to do when he was a grown-up but there was one thing he was sure of. "Daddy, when I am older, I will make a lot of money." I beamed. Now was my chance to give my son one of those life-changing, enlightening lectures about the merits of working hard to get what you want out of life. I was about to explain that if you do something you love then you won't ever really work a day in your life. I was also going to have the privilege of explaining to my child that nothing can ever beat hard work. If you work

81

hard and get the job done you will always sleep well at night. I was going to tie all of these mini symposiums into one speech that would have lasted the last three miles or so to the park. I adjusted my rearview mirror to make eye contact.

Then I said, "Do you know how you get a lot of money, son?" I looked at him real serious so he would know I was about to drop some major knowledge on him. Then I asked him again for emphasis. "Do you know how you get a lot of money, son?"

He met my eyes in the mirror and said, "Yes. First, I will go to the wallet store and buy a really big wallet."

I asked him why and he said, "The bigger my wallet is, the more money I will be able to put inside of it."

Oh, yeah. That works, too. Again, I couldn't argue with him. If you want a lot of money, you better get yourself a big wallet.

I once asked Jackie, "Did you poop yet today?"

He answered, "Maybe."

When I asked him what he meant by "maybe," he said, "I said 'maybe' so I won't be lying."

Again he was right. Do you remember if *you* pooped today? Maybe.

Children are very honest. They are very strange and very honest. One night I was changing Jackie's diaper.

He said to me, "Daddy, I don't like babies."

He was barely three at the time so I was amused at his separating himself from the lowly baby class. I asked him why he didn't like babies and he just shrugged and said, "Because I am the pits."

The next day after preschool, Nik and I took Jackie out for ice cream. While we were in the ice-cream shop a woman walked in with a stroller. In the stroller was a newborn baby. Jackie looked into the stroller and then asked the woman, "Is that your baby?"

The lady thought it was so cute. A three-year-old, arms covered in ice cream, asking her baby questions.

Jackie continued: "Is your baby a boy?"

The woman told him yes.

Then he pointed in at the infant's beautiful little feet and asked, "Are those his tootsies?"

The woman was now glowing with pride. She bent down so her face was closer to Jackson's. She said softly to him, "Yes, those are his tootsies." She smiled.

Jackie leaned in closer to her face so they were now practically nose to nose and said, "I don't like babies." Then he walked away and sat at a table across the ice-cream shop.

I already knew that Jackie didn't like babies but I have to admit that I was thrilled with the way he set the lady up! Each question he asked her, he asked her very gently. He even got the lady to lean in closer to him so he could whisper his baby opinion like the Bad Seed.

Toddlers have the ability to be very logical. They can be analytical and again, always brutally honest. They will never pass up a chance to say "Look how fat she is!" regarding the woman next to you in line at the bank. A three-year-old has the compulsion to tell you "He has brown skin!" about the loan officer sitting across from you.

One day Nik and I were walking Jackie to school and a homeless man ambled past us mumbling to himself. Nik and I kept our heads down and ignored him. Not the boy. No, instead my kid practically held on to the homeless guy's jacket to keep him in place and asked, "Daddy, is this man crazy?"

I was mortified.

The homeless man looked up at Nik as if to say, "Aw hell, let's call a spade a spade," and shuffled off.

So Nik looked at Jackie and said, "Yes, honey, this man is crazy. But not as crazy as we are!"

The homeless guy gave the three of us a little wave and shuffled up the street. Jackie didn't really do anything extraordinary. What he was asking wasn't some oddly taboo question. We never established the sanity of the homeless population with him. So it stands to reason that a reasonable mind would want to know definitively, "Is this man crazy?"

Why are adults so embarrassed by these questions? Why do we cringe when children say, "Look, that man has no legs!"?

It's because they are being honest. They are asking what we are all thinking. We constantly tell our children, "Don't stare!" Well, I ask you—what the hell is the difference between a child staring and a grown-up who says they really love "people watching"? In my opinion, "people watching" is ruder. (But if a lady weighs four hundred pounds, I should be able to stare at her in the bakery aisle. She earned it.)

One of the great things about kids' logic is their ability to do exceedingly bizarre things and make them seem, well, logical. When Jackson was three and a half, I put him down for a much-needed nap. This in and of itself was a blessing that I took for granted at the time. Babies don't really plan out their naps; they just pass out and don't wake up for a few hours. When Jackie was two, three, almost four, he would take a nap every day. When he was three he could really bang out some long, quality naps. Pretty much all 365 days of his third year on earth he napped. Usually his naps were two or three hours long. This was special. If he was napping, that meant that I could take a nap. My naps are usually only an hour so I still had two hours to play Play-Station before Jackie woke up. After sleeping deeply for three hours, he would wake up and look like a heroin junkie on a weeks-long bender. He would be all wet from sweating through his clothes (drugs?). His hair would be standing straight up and he would be completely confused. But for some reason, as soon as Jackie turned four, the naps ended. This was a sad day. Gone were my own daily naps and taking the Jets to the Super Bowl on Madden. Not only did my son stop taking naps but he also refused to even admit to being tired. The poor guy would have a head cold for two weeks. He would go to preschool and play like a psychopath with his little buddies. He would be slurring his speech in the car ride home. Sometimes I would look in the rearview mirror and catch him holding his eyelids open with his thumbs.

Nik would ask him, "Honey boy, are you sleepy?"

Jackie would drop his hands into his lap and say simply, "No."

It's very hard to convince a four-year-old that he is tired. He just denies and denies and denies it. For a kid to say the words "I'm tired" is the equivalent of a navy SEAL saying, "I surrender." I tried everything to get my kid to nap. I would tell him he couldn't go outside unless he napped. He wouldn't nap. He would then spend the next few hours very happily in the house with his Legos and cars. I told him that if he took a nap, I would take him to the zoo when he woke up. He didn't nap. We didn't go to the zoo. He didn't care. Sometimes I would even *instruct* him to nap. No excuses. Nap . . . or else! He didn't nap. I haven't really established what "or else" means, though, so after he flopped around in the bed for a half hour I turned the light on in his room and we watched *The Powerpuff Girls* together. The fact of the matter was that for some reason, Jackie was adamantly against napping. Could it be that once when he was napping I ducked out and caught a Dodgers game? Maybe. The game being a doubleheader probably didn't help. At least I brought him back a giant foam finger to cry into. (I need to let child services know that I am joking here. It wasn't a double-header.)

One day, shortly after lunch, I put Jackie down for a nap that he did not want to take. After I got him under his blankets, I took out my cell phone and pretended to call every park within a twenty-mile radius of our house. I told each park to stay closed for the next two hours because Jackie Mohr was taking a nap and no one should be allowed to play while he was sleeping. I pretended to call three toy stores. I fake-called all of our neighbors with kids and confirmed that their children were napping now, too. It didn't work.

I learned a valuable lesson that year. You cannot force someone to sleep. All you do is increase their anxiety about not being able to sleep and make it worse. My advice to parents with a similar problem would be to buy Benadryl strips. Give your daughter a Benadryl strip and then put her in the car and drive in a straight line for as long as possible.

When your child asks, "Where are we going?" tell her you want to see how long you can drive without stopping.

Eventually she will feel helpless and surrender to her body's wish and doze off. For about three minutes. Then of course you have to drive an hour home with a newly awake, cranky child.

Can you imagine not wanting to take a nap? It is inconfuckingceivable. There will never, ever, be a day in my life where if the opportunity to knock down for twenty minutes presents itself I won't jump at it. I can nap on chairs, beds, backyards, the beach, cars, planes, and floors. Some people have trouble sleeping. I have trouble staying awake. If you put me in a movie theater, good night. If you tell me supper will be ready in half an hour, I will utilize that half hour to stare at the back of my eyelids. I laugh when people tell me they can't sleep on airplanes. What the hell else are you going to do? Watch an Ashton Kutcher movie? Sudoku?

Jackie doesn't sleep on planes, either. If you give him a Matchbox car and a Q-tip, he will kill two hours.

One day I told him that if he took a nap I would take him for a bike ride around the reservoir when he woke up. God was smiling down on me. Jackie not only agreed to take the nap but he fell asleep, too! I was stunned. I quickly went into my bedroom and closed my eyes so I could nap as well. About an hour and a half later I heard through the baby monitor, "Daddy, I'm done with my nap."

I got up and padded across the house to pull him from his crib. When I put the light on in his room, my boy was standing up in his crib, smiling and ready to greet me. It was sweet. It was also incredibly strange. Jackie had the zipper to his onesie pulled all the way down in the front to the top of his diaper. He looked very Elvis-like with his giant V-neck and flipped-up collar. He also was covered in a white substance. I mean he was *covered*. His hair was slicked back with it and it was all over his face and down the V-neck across his chest and covering his belly. Even the backs of his hands were covered and white. The only part of his body not covered was his eyes. In fact there were two perfect circles around his eyes where he did not apply the mystery goo.

I asked him, "Jackie, what did you do?"

He explained to me very excitedly, "Don't worry, Daddy, I was careful of my eyes!"

I was beyond confused. I scanned the baby room and the surrounding area of his crib. That's when I spotted a now-empty bottle of baby lotion on his diaper changer. The cap was off and what was once inside the bottle was now covering my child from head to belly. With of course the exception of two large perfect circles around his peepers.

When Jackie had woken up, he had leaned out of his crib and reached onto the diaper changing station and grabbed the lotion bottle. He then lathered himself up really good and even slicked back his hair. I asked him why he did it and he told me, "I didn't want to get a sunborn, Daddy. Don't worry though I was careful of my eyes! I didn't want to get a sunborn. I didn't want to wake you up, so I did it. I was careful of my eyes!"

With his white skin, big, spooky eyes, and slicked-back hair, he looked like a cross between Casper the Friendly Ghost and a Guido from the Jersey shore. A deal is a deal, though, so I loaded up the truck with our bikes and we went to the reservoir. I didn't wipe any of the layers of baby lotion off his face or body. He looked too awesome. Neither Nik nor I had the heart to point out to the boy that it was a cloudy day. It didn't matter. My son, true to his word, did not get a sunborn. And as always, he was careful of his eyes. I would easily pay a hundred thousand dollars to relive that afternoon.

Kids also *lose* all sense of logic sometimes and no more so than when it comes to animals. Do not, under any circumstance, buy a pet for your child. Don't ever buy them dogs. Don't ever buy them kittens. Don't buy them any goldfish or hamsters or snakes or birds. The reason for this is simple. In two weeks (if you're lucky), that pet will be all yours. Your child won't even remember the dog's name let alone remember to take it out to piss and shit. Kids are terrified of dog shit. You have a better chance of training your dog to crap on the toilet than you do of having your child clean up dog shit with a plastic bag.

Kids are horrible dog walkers, too. They drop the leash about six or seven times a block and they try to break the dog's neck by jerking the leash too hard. When the dog wants to sniff, they demand that the dog start jogging. When the dog wants to run a little, they demand that the dog sit and stay for no reason whatsoever. When children do take an interest in the family dog for longer than a month or so, they tend to do horrible damage to the animal. Anytime you walk past a neighbor's house and their dog starts barking like a freaking maniac, that dog had too many kids in its life. Dogs that constantly hump or bite or bark all the time are usually the victims of child-to-animal abuse.

When it comes to pets, kids really suck. They will make your cats never come out from under the bed. They will teach your parrot to curse out your grandmother. And also, whatever you do, don't let your children name your pets. Kids are absolutely horrible at naming pets. If you don't believe me, ask your 140-pound chocolate Labrador named "Puppy." You let the kids name that thing, didn't you? We're all guilty of it at one point or another. No animal escapes unscathed. I asked Jackie to name a goldfish and he named it . . . wait for it . . . Goldie.

Goldie lived to be about six months old. He had a great five-month run but then I handed the feeding duties to my kid. A month later, Goldie was deadie.

You can tell what dogs in the neighborhood were named by the kids of the house. It's always a white dog named Snowball or a black Lab named Blackie. All the good names for dogs and cats are people names. I like a Rottweiler named Shirley or a Tabby named Norman. Shirley and Norman would totally kick the shit out of Blackie and Snowball.

I like the name Shirley so much for a Rottie, that I even had one of my very own. She was a great dog and I guess Jackie thought so, too, because he liked to put his fingers in her ass. Now, Shirley was a huge dog, and at the time her ass was about chest level with my four-year-old. One day the dog backed up a little bit within arm's reach of Jackie and he saw it as an opportunity to plug the old girl's poop chute with his index finger. My reaction was completely wrong. Instead of acting like nothing out of the ordinary was happening, I burst out laughing and told my friend, "Get over here and look at this!" I automatically knew my reaction was the worst one possible, judging by the look of glee on Jackie's face as he reloaded and refired. The dog wasn't exactly helping the situation. She must have liked it because she kept backing up to help him insert his finger.

There is a lesson here. As parents, we know how to act in certain situations. But I believe that we should really be practicing how to *react*. I lie in my bed at night and wonder what I would say if Jackie asked me a certain question or did a particularly amusing stunt. I always try to think ahead to strange scenarios and ask myself what the best reaction would be. Action is easy. Reaction is tricky. It is also tricky, not to mention bizarre, to lie in bed and wonder, "Okay, what will I say if my kid sticks his finger in my dog's ass?"

One arena where the "action is easy" theory gets tough is swearing. Me and my big mouth have a difficult time with this one. Once a baby enters the home, we have about a one-year shelf life on our swear words. Some kids begin to talk earlier than others so you may have to monitor the time limit as you go. For example, if at one year old your son is asking you, "Daddy, do you think since the end of the cold war, NATO is proving to be obsolete?" you must stop swearing immediately. If your child is like mine and gurgles until he is two and a half years old, swear while you still can.

Nonetheless, it is no easy transition. I, for one, have a mouth like a truck driver. So do all of my friends and Nik. I never realized how filthy my language was until my son arrived. On the telephone, in the car (oh my God, in the car!), watching television. These are all activities that I had not realized were incomplete without a few choice four-letter bombs.

I walk a tightrope all week long, depending on whether Jackie is around. Whatever you swear and whenever you swear, children have an uncanny ability to identify the words you used as priceless nuggets to be used later, usually when you have company over. I was an unfortunate witness to this phenomenon when Jackie was about three and a half and I had workmen over installing some new appliances in the kitchen.

As the men jockeyed the appliances through the house, my son blurted out, "Daddy, I'm a fucker!"

"Excuse me?"

He obliged with "I'm a fucker!"

Thinking quick on my feet, I said, "Well, hello, falcon, I am an eagle." Then before he could respond, I added, "Are you sure you are a falcon? Because eagles are so cool."

"No, I am a falcon."

Phew! Major party foul avoided.

Or so I thought.

A few hours passed and Jackie was playing with a few toy

cars on the couch when he looked up and yelled, "I am going to fuck the basement!"

"What?" I knew what he said but I couldn't believe what I heard.

"I am going to fuck the basement!" This time he yelled it with a rather large smile on his face. I didn't know how to work *falcon* back into this version of his eloquence so I calmly told him, "We do not have a basement." I then started to walk away, hoping this bit of rationale would satisfy him. No such luck.

"Get a basement, Daddy! I will fuck it!"

Where in the book does it tell you how to respond to a request for the purchase or construction of a basement for the purpose of having sex with it? There is no such manual and if there were, I am pretty sure the pages of it would be filled with advice on how to bring down a fever and avoid diaper rash. I am fairly certain that it would not have a chapter on "Basement Fucking."

God as my witness, I have never, ever, mentioned having sex with my basement—in front of my child or otherwise. I have never called myself a fucker. The logical thing to do after hearing obscenities from your child is to wonder where he may have heard them. The simple answer is that your child no doubt heard them from you. In my case my son not only heard the swear words from me but also felt free to improvise their context and tense. It is much easier to think of the kids your child has playdates with and assign blame to them and their no-good parents, but in the end, deep down inside, you know it was you.

Later that same day, after the nanny told me Jackie was yelling, "You fucker!" to cars as they passed by on the street outside, I knew I had to sit down and speak with him. I told him that the words he was using were bad-boy words and bad boys get spanked. Jackie somberly nodded his head and went back to his cars.

After our discussion, I turned on the television to watch some TiVo'd *Bob the Builder* with my boy. As the television came on, I rooted around for the remote and heard a crystal-clear "You fuckers!" come from the still-dark screen. My son looked up at me as if to say, "Now what do we do?"

I spent the next five minutes acting like a fool and miming spanking the television screen, which was now on mute.

7

TRADITION

Your child's birthday is always a blast. All any kid cares about is the presents. Like looting pirates, they have but one mission and it's to secure as much booty as humanly possible and secure it in a private place in their bedroom. Don't you hate how other kids always try to play with your kid's toys at his party? The balls on these kids must be the size of Gibraltar. "Hey, pal, he just got this freaking thing. Back off!" Don't these kids know how to behave at a party? Sit down, have some cake, and treat my son like royalty. It's the unwritten law of birthday parties. How come some kids never received the memo on this one? What's the deal with some asshole kid thinking he has the right to "help" blow out the candles? It's always someone's younger child. Usually around age two. All the adults giggle and make remarks about how cute it is that the little guy blew out the candles. Yeah, real cute. My child, on his birthday, put every fiber of his being into a wish and some chubby prick just blew it. Literally.

As a little boy, I would become enraged if someone messed with my cake. I enjoyed the pageantry of it all. Everyone was completely focused on me as a beautiful cake with one more candle than the year before was carefully cradled into the room by my mom. Everyone would sing and I would stare down at the cake, thinking fast on my feet as to what my wish would be. The birthday wish seems to always have been the one thing I forgot to lock down every year. I made sure the invitations went out and I told my friends at school about how great the party was going to be. I picked out the outfit I wanted to wear days before and combed my hair to perfection the morning of, even going so far as to use a little of my dad's Brylcreem for styling. I carefully planned out who would sit where and how much time I would spend with each guest. I knew well in advance what toys I wanted and mapped out how and where I would play with them if I got what I asked for. I knew which friend would be the most fun for each toy, too. Then the cake comes out and someone yells "Make a wish!" and I would draw a blank. Every year. I would try to think as fast as I could for a fitting wish. My presents were already purchased so it was futile to wish for something I hadn't received. I didn't want to waste a wish on a toy for the next year's party because who knew what I would want a year from now. Visions of a trip to Disney World or

Six Flags would rifle through my head and I would keep spinning the Rolodex of wishes in my head until I came up with a good one.

The last thing I needed was some asshole blowing out my candles while I was thinking of a wish, so the pressure was really on. Inevitably, though, during this time of great concentration, some kid at the party would seize the opportunity to dig a finger into my cake or try to blow out my candles. If the offending party was successful at either of these horrible tricks the cake became immediately inedible. Who wants a birthday cake with your neighbor's thumbprint in it? Not me. Cake time was officially over and it was time to go play with my new toys.

Some adults could prove to be inept at birthday parties, as well. Every year, one of my friend's parents would give me a toy and not have the common courtesy to include batteries. Were they serious? Didn't they see the commercials where the voice-over guy says "batteries not included" and "parts sold separately" super fast at the end? It was never a toy you were blasé about, either. The toy that came without batteries was always the mother of all presents for that year. Usually a remote-controlled car or something equally important.

If kids could plan and run their own birthday parties there would be a few rules changed. Number one would be *no cards!* Ugh. Every year you get handed a monster-size box with a picture of Hot Wheels on it and your mom would say, "Open the card!" Why? What the hell good is that going to do? Unless there is some serious cash in the card I am just going to fake like I'm reading it anyway. That's what I did with the last fifteen cards I was forced to open! Words. That's what is in those cards. Just stupid words. They always said the same thing, too. "Happy Birthday." Whoopee! A card that says "Happy Birthday!" This is the greatest party ever. I am reading! Blech. That might be interesting, but I can't read. Why are you making me open the cards when I can't read? Are you mocking me?

On Jackie's fourth birthday party, he surprised me. As I pulled the card off of one of his presents, he shouted, "Open the card!"

I was confused. I asked, "Why?"

He said, "Because I can't read . . . I thought you knew that."

My son likes cards. What a strange dude.

The other big rule change that would happen if kids ran their own parties is that presents would be opened upon *arrival*. None of this opening presents at the end of the party garbage. What good does that do? The kid gets everyone crowded around, opens all the presents, and then fifteen minutes later, everybody goes home. Nothing is more fun than playing Ping-Pong by yourself. I've seen it done in cartoons before but the players all seemed to have super speed, compared to me. I could never get around to the other side of the table fast enough to return my own serve. The faster I tried to run to the other side, the greater my chances were of whacking my ribs on the table's pointy corners.

In a perfect world, gifts wouldn't even be wrapped. People would show up and hand you your toys the minute they got out of their cars. Any clothing you received would be handed to your mother and promptly put in the dresser, never to be mentioned again. Any child caught trying to finger someone else's cake would be spanked, with their pants around their ankles, in front of all the other kids. Cards would not exist and parents that brought toys without batteries would immediately be sent back to the store to get them. Same thing goes with presents that need assembling. Put the goddamn Big Wheel together before you come to the house!

Parents would also no longer be allowed to make time-sensitive jokes on your birthday. Every year, as a kid, on my birthday I would spring out of bed and dash into the dining room and tell everyone that the birthday boy had awakened. Every year, without fail, my parents would look groggily up from their coffee and tell me I wasn't born until four-thirty in the afternoon so technically it wasn't my birthday yet. Hilarious. A regular Stiller and Meara.

Another big rule change, and this is a big one: You cannot punish a kid for using a toy properly. If someone gets me a pistol that shoots disks or pellets, they should fully expect me to shoot someone in the face with it. After all, it's my party and my present. What if the kid I shot tried to "help" me blow out my candles? His parents thought it was cute but I thought a party foul of that magnitude needed to be met with a little frontier justice. Why the hell would you buy me a gun unless you expected me to shoot someone with it? What was I supposed to use it for? Guns are for shooting! If you don't want to feel the wrath of the young gun-slinging birthday boy then I suggest you get your ass to a different party.

Jackie had his third birthday party at Chuck E. Cheese's. You are certainly aware of Chuck E. Cheese's, since they litter the landscape almost as predominantly as McDonald's and Sears. I cannot possibly give Chuck E. Cheese's a high enough recommendation. Forget the zoo, forget the pool, and get your kid into Chuck E. Cheese's for his next party. Chuck E. Cheese's is like Las Vegas for kids. They party hard at the Chuck. There is dancing, singing, pizza, and most importantly, *more toys!* The place is filled with games like Skee-Ball and Whac-A-Mole. Each time you finish playing one of these games, the machine spits out a few little tickets. Each ticket you receive puts you closer to your ultimate goal. More stuff! For only a thousand tickets you can bring home a nice plastic bracelet, rubber ball, or a ring with an ant on it. Kids know this and they become degenerate gamblers at Chuck E. Cheese's. Jackie had his hair combed super handsomely and he was wearing an adorable outfit when we got to the Chuck for his party. Two hours later he looked like Jim from *Taxi*. He was covered in sweat and had stains all over the front of his shirt. He was drooling and in every picture his eyes are half closed like he was on a bender. Chuck E. Cheese's is actually better than Las Vegas. All the kids leave with the same amount of money they came in with—zero.

One ritual that Nik and I desperately want to pass on to Jackson is our belief in a higher power. I had months of anxiety about how boring he would find church services or whether he would care at all about sitting through a mass and becoming a member of a parish. Thankfully, we've never had a problem convincing Jackson to come to church with us. Through our priest and friend, Father Tim, we felt as if we had found the perfect person to extend a hand toward our six-year-old. For a few weeks we gave Jackie the hard sell, telling him, "Father Tim surfs!" or "Father Tim is younger than Daddy!"

So we set up a day to bring Jackie to St. Monica's and show him around. It was a bit like a recruiting visit for me. I wanted my boy to really love this church. I wanted him to be baptized in this church. My wife was baptized in this church. Nik showed Jackie around and taught him how to properly apply holy water and make the sign of the cross. This was a huge hit. If you want to impress a six-year-old, tell him that they are touching actual holy water. I thought that the holy water would have sealed the deal as far as Jackie liking the church but we kept the tour of divinity going. We knelt in the pews and put our hands together and prayed in the giant, empty church. We could hear each other breathing. I finished first and then Nik stood up. As I looked down at Jackie praying, I was a bit overcome. I mindlessly put my hand on top of his head. My son, mistaking my loving gesture as a sign to "wrap it up," squinted his eyes harder shut and said loudly, "I'm not done!" A few seconds later he opened his eyes and performed a hybrid version of crossing himself and swatting a fly.

After taking the church tour and applying holy water a few more times before we left (for good measure), Jackie made it very clear to me and Nik that he wanted to be baptized at St. Monica's. We told him that this was wonderful news. We asked him what he thought a baptism meant. He then explained, with odd clarity, that baptism is forgiveness for everything that a person did or could do wrong. He went on to say that being baptized is like being welcomed into a church. He kind of nailed it.

Jackson's first Catholic mass at St. Monica's was *mostly* a success. He loved the part where you turn and shake your neighbors' hands and say, "good morning." He really hammed it up and worked his way up and down the aisles. He also liked the end of the homily when the priest told us all to shake each other's hands and say "Peace be with you." The forty minutes in between were a little harder for him to focus. The monsignor's homily that morning was about Jesus's willingness to touch the sick and the wretched. The lesson basically being that we should all take time out of our day to spend a little quality time with people less fortunate than ourselves. The monsignor said, "Jesus broke the law in the temple." Jackie snapped to attention and asked a little too loudly, "Jesus broke the law?" I told him in the softest whisper I could muster that I would explain all of it to him when we left. The monsignor followed up Jesus' breaking the law with the story of Jesus rebuking the evil spirit in the temple. Jackie said even louder now, "There was an evil spirit?" Then "What does rebuke mean?" Again I told him that I would explain all of it to him after mass. I handed him a pencil and a donation envelope and told him to draw (exactly what my mother used to do with me). When mass was over I told Jackie that the man in the temple was filled with an evil spirit and Jesus broke the law by touching him and rebuking the spirit. His blank stare let me know that I wasn't doing a good job translating the day's homily to a child.

Eventually I explained to him, "Jesus has the force. Jesus is the Jedi Knight. The man in the temple was on the dark side and Jesus used the Force to bring the man over to the good side and back into the Federation." Jackie paused for a second and let out a huge smile. He said, "I didn't know Jesus knew the Force!" I explained to him not only that Jesus knew the Force but also that "Holy Ghost" was another name for the Force. My son had had a vision in his head of a guy covered in a sheet running up and down church hallways yelling, "Wooooo wooooo!" He was pretty relieved to know that the Holy Ghost was just the Force.

It was shortly before Christmas of 2008 when I received a call from Father Tim inviting Nik, Jackie, and me to come down to the church and help out for their annual "Dinner for the less fortunate." We were thrilled about the invite as this was our opportunity to follow through with what we learned at mass and spend more time with those who are less fortunate. The only problem was that we were in the middle of preparing for our own annual family Christmas dinner. Nik was up to her neck in shrimp salads and baking turnovers for our family, who were scheduled to arrive at around four that afternoon. Nik and I decided that I'd go with Jackie to St. Monica's to help out with the dinner for the less fortunate and come home around three to make sure we were home in time to greet the family.

Jackie was playing Legos when I told him that Father Tim had called and invited us down to the church to help people less fortunate than we were. I figured that Jackie's love of Legos would override my love of Christ and he would beg to get out of going, but to my wonderful surprise, my son acted like it was the best phone call a kid could receive short of one from Santa Claus. We both quickly changed into more presentable church attire. As I was helping my son into his cowboy boots, I was struck by the most wondrous thought: I am dressing my son up for church! Nik was disappointed that she would not be able to make it over to St. Monica's that afternoon. So was I. She makes everything more fun. On our way out the door she told me, "Please tell Father Tim that I'm sorry I can't be there. Tell him I am stuck here making dinner for the *too* fortunate." She kissed her boys and we were off.

We found Father Tim in the stairwell of the gymnasium, speaking perfect Spanish to a group of families. He had a master's in divinity and used it daily in two languages. Show-off. He saw Jackie and me and gave us a very warm greeting. Upon meeting Father Tim personally for the first time, Jackie decided to forgo the cursory handshake as a greeting and instead threw his arms around our priest in a giant hug. Father Tim hugged him right back and thanked him for coming. He told us to follow him into the gymnasium and he would put us to work. What struck me instantly about the inside of the gym was how calm it was. Here there were more than six hundred people being given free meals and no one was shoving or pushing. No one was raising their voice. It was pleasant and organized. Jackie and I were given name tags to wear and then waited for our job assignment. I wondered whether we would be giving out slices of turkey or scoops of mashed potatoes. Father Tim then handed us both a couple of thirty-gallon trash bags. He said, "You guys can go pick up trash for a while. Just clear the dirty dishes from the tables and when your bag is full, bring it back here."

Trash duty. Perfect. Symbolically, what could be more appropriate for our entrance into the Catholic Church? In the business world it would be the equivalent of starting in the mailroom. Where else would I start? Former first lady of California Maria Shriver and her brothers were handing out the turkey and mashed potatoes. They had belonged to this parish since before I was born.

Jackie and I began working our way up and down the rows of long tables in the gymnasium, picking up trash. My kid held his trash bag open and asked each family, "Basura? Basura?" (*Basura* means "trash" in Spanish.) Jackie was on a roll. He asked each table, "Basura?" and they put their trash into his bag and said, "Gracias." He then said, "De nada." It was surprising and precious. I took my cue from Jackie and started asking each family as I passed, "Basura? Basura?" I was filled with pride. I was filled with the Holy Spirit. I was filled with confusion. Where the hell did my son learn to speak Spanish?

We placed our trash bags into a large bin and Father Tim handed Jackie and me trays with paper bowls of peanuts in them. Our next job was to hand out peanuts to the people in the gymnasium. Still buzzing from speaking Spanish to the families while picking up garbage, I asked Father Tim what the Spanish word for peanuts was. He replied, "Cacahuetes." I asked him again and again he said, "Cacahuetes." I asked him to slow it down and say it to me phonetically. He obliged and slowly, as if speaking to a six-year-old, said, "Ka-ka-WAT-tays." I looked at Father Tim and said, "I'm not saying that." I wanted to be a good Catholic and have a church to call my own but at some point a man just has to put his foot down. Instead I went from table to table like a Dodger Stadium vendor hollering "Peanuts! Peanuts!"

I wasn't going to look other adults in the eyes and say "Ka-ka-WAT-tays."

The peanuts weren't as big a hit as the trash. People were much more excited to give us garbage than they were to receive cacahuetes. When our trays were emptied and void of peanuts, Father Tim walked us out and we spoke for a little while longer in the church parking lot. I remembered to tell Father Tim that Nik couldn't come because she was "preparing dinner for the too fortunate." He smiled and said, "Hey, that's important, too. That's family, bro."

As we said our good-byes, Jackie kept hugging Father Tim. Whenever there was a pause in the conversation or whenever we took a few steps to leave, he kept jogging back for a hug. I would say that Father Tim and Jackson shared about a half-dozen hugs in that five minutes alone. Jackie said, "I hope you have the best day ever in the whole entire universe!" Father Tim seemed to really like this blessing. He called Jackie's name and motioned for him to come back toward him. Jackie again jogged up to the priest, hugged him (naturally), and listened with great interest to what his priest said next. Tim looked at him and said, "Hey, brother, let's make a deal. You pray for me and I'll pray for you, okay?"

Jackie said, "It's a deal. Let's shake on it." The two shook hands and after one last hug, Jackie jogged back to me with a profoundly happy smile on his face. As we were about to get in the car, Jackie asked if we could hurry back inside to light a candle. I obliged. We both clumsily put our fingers into the holy water and crossed ourselves. I made a very deliberate and slow cross, making sure I was doing it right, in case Jackie was watching. We walked over to the candles and prayed. When I was finished, I pushed the button to the candle that I wanted to light. Jackson walked over to a candle, closed his eyes, prayed, and then pushed the button. We both left church feeling like a million bucks.

Later, as I was clicking Jackie into his car seat, I was so emotional. I was overflowing with good cheer and gratitude. I looked at Jackson and said, "I love you and I am so proud of you." He grabbed my head and pinned it to his face and said, "You are the best daddy ever. I love you." It was then that I thought of how amazing a day my son and I had just had. I also remembered what Father Tim told Jackie about praying for him. I said, "Hey, we're supposed to pray for Father Tim! Let's pray for Father Tim." My son put his hand to his mouth like he was telling a secret and said, "That's who I prayed for when I lit my candle."

8

PARENTHOOD HAS ITS
ADVANTAGES

I have found that being a parent brings with it an enormous set
of privileges. I could go on and on about how being a dad has
made me a more patient man. I could wax poetic about how
the doors of love have flung themselves open, revealing to me a
world of beauty heretofore unimaginable. I won't.

I will, however, let you in on what I realized early on was the
single most rewarding part of having a baby. *Carpool Lane!* This
may not seem to warrant such a high ranking on the priority list
but believe me, every parent in Southern California reading this
book just wisely nodded their head in agreement.

In Los Angeles, the traffic is so bad, you might actually be better off tooling around on a bicycle in Hong Kong. There have been days that I sat on the 405, completely still, for so long that I have actually put the car in park and closed my eyes for a nap. The carpool lane is always there, mocking me. People in the carpool lane fly past the rest of us while laughing and singing, at speeds breaking the sound barrier. Motorcycles have it good in L.A., too. They weave haphazardly in and out and around traffic that has otherwise completely ground to a halt. Some days it takes every fiber of my being as a good citizen to not throw open my car door as one of these bikers flies by. Trust me, it's harder than you think. If I sent a motorcycle driver sailing through the sky and watched him fall with a thud on someone else's windshield, I would at least have something to do for the next forty-five minutes. I would get out to see if he was okay, then the cops would come and there would be copious amounts of paperwork to fill out. That would kill a good portion of time. If the accident I caused was bad enough, I might actually spend enough time at the scene of the accident for traffic to clear up and I could do a good eighty miles per hour the rest of the way home. At the very least, because of the carnage I caused, the other side of the freeway would become its own parking lot as rubberneckers slowed down to gawk at the dying motorcycle man. I would take pride in this. I would get out of my car and wave to all the motorists who found themselves in gridlock and smile at the fact that at least everyone on both sides of the freeway was stationary for a reason. Maybe I could open the door and send the motorcycle guy flying into the air. Maybe he could land on his back in the carpool lane and get run over by a van with only two people in it.

The strange thing about having a baby in the carpool lane is that it takes a few months to realize that your child actually counts as a person. How strange. My kid is only twelve pounds and I can use him to carpool? He doesn't even face the front of the car! If you say so, officer, I will drive in the carpool lane with my tiny person who can't drive himself regardless, so it's not a technical "carpool" in the true sense of the word.

The rules for carpooling in Los Angeles dictate that you must have two or more persons in your car to use the left lane, the carpool lane. Too many times to remember I have been sitting in bumper-to-bumper traffic with my 110-pound Rottweiler, thinking how unfair it is that tiny ninety-five-pound people were flying past me in the carpool lane. But no matter how small your child is, he counts! I encourage you to drive as fast as you like and laugh at the overweight people sitting in their cars as you and a person who can't even hold his own head up sail past.

While I am on the subject of the carpool lane, what's with the asshole who keeps driving the actual speed limit while in the carpool lane? Who is he, the hall monitor? "Sixty-five is the limit and no one is getting past me." Jerks.

It's always the same car, too. It's always some powder-blue Toyota Tercel with the tint on the back window all screwed up and bubbly. There is always some geographic-pride bumper sticker on the car that says "I love El Salvador!" Now get out from in front of me and my lil' carpool buddy, would ya! I have to get home. He's waking up! It's just not right to drive the speed limit in the carpool lane. When you drive in the carpool lane it should look like *Tron!*

Driving with three-year-olds can be treacherous. The DVD player is both a godsend and a hazard for parents. It's like baby Xanax. Twenty minutes into *Dora the Explorer* and the kid nods off like a narcoleptic. Many SUVs, minivans, and cars are blessed with a DVD player in them. The problem is that the monitor is behind the driver. There is nothing like a six-hour drive up the coast with a constant barrage of "Look! Daddy, look!" Or more dangerous is the almighty "What's that?"

I may be oversimplifying. It is usually more along the lines of "What's that? What's that? Daddy? What's that? What's that? Look! What's that? What's that? What's that?"

I may be oversimplifying still. After about a steady half hour of "What's that?" I start to wonder, What the hell *is* that? Why is he so confused? What movie did I put in for this kid, *Vanilla Sky?*

Inevitably, my curiosity gets the better of me and I will crane my neck back and upward to catch a glimpse of what my kid is watching (even though I know what he's watching because I'm the one who put it in for him). This is bad news for every other motorist out there. It isn't the safest thing to do. Try it and see how many times, when you settle your eyes back on the road, you are moments from being wedged into someone else's trunk. For the sake of avoiding litigation, I must say this has absolutely never happened to me. Ever. If you think you were rear-ended by a black Cadillac Escalade, license plate SPNGBOB, you weren't. Stop being so paranoid.

Often the best conversations I have with Jackie take place in the car. The types of cars on the road are of the utmost importance. He categorizes and files each and every vehicle that comes on his radar.

"What kind of car is that?"

"That is a Chevy."

"What kind of car is that?"

"That's a Chevy, too."

"Two Chevys?"

"No, I meant that car is also a Chevy."

"Also a Chevy, Daddy?"

"Yes, sir."

"What does *also* mean?"

"It means that there are two Chevys."

"Two Chevys, Daddy?"

"Uh . . . yeah."

He got me.

I find it sad when parents get annoyed with the conversations they have with their children. Some of Jackie's most rewarding material has been said while we were driving, shooting the shit. When Jackie was three, he and I were driving home from a friend's house and after a long silence he asked, "Are you happy, Daddy?"

Wow. Well, how could I not be? He asked this with such sincerity in his voice that tears actually welled up in my eyes. I looked at him in the rearview mirror and asked, "Did you just ask me if I was happy?"

"Yes."

"I am *so* happy and I love you so much!"

"I love you so much, Daddy."

"Are you just repeating what I said or do you really, really love your daddy?"

"I love you, Daddy. I love you very."

Enough said.

I try to engage in as much conversation with Jackie as possible for the simple reason that I wish my father had done it more with me. Again the theory of escalating love comes in. I will answer any and all questions my child asks. I enjoy the challenge that comes with my son asking a billion questions that I have to put all my cynicism aside to try to answer in a way that a three-year-old will not only understand, but remember. I can also gauge my child's level of exhaustion by the questions he asks. Jackie will be on one of his car inquiries and after asking me the make and model of each and every car that passes, he will start asking what color the cars are. This line of questioning can only mean one thing. Nap time.

I admit that I have it easy since I have only one child. I cannot imagine being in a long car ride with four kids, all asking a million questions in between their arguments with one another. So one child it is for me (so far) and I look forward to our car discussions.

Interestingly enough, many of the most memorable conversations I've had with my father were also in the car, and some of my earliest memories are of him and me driving around our little town in Verona, New Jersey, in his convertible Spitfire. Now, as an adult, I think my father's dry sense of humor is great. As a child though, the dryness, as well as any irony, usually got lost in translation. Sometimes my father would say things that he found amusing but inevitably made me cry.

I remember when I was about six, my family and I were driving in our gray station wagon to my father's company picnic. I didn't know it when we first got in the car but my father's office was two hours from our house. About thirty minutes into the drive I asked the front of the car, "How much longer?"

My father answered with a reassuring "Just over the next hill."

We were driving up a long, winding hill at the time, so I set my body clock to the information I had just been given. When we reached the top of the hill, I could see nothing but farmland

and open sky in front of us. I didn't mention it at the moment because I figured we would simply turn off the road at any time and pull into a gravelly parking lot and I would be looking at pony rides, sack races, and hot dogs as soon as we parked. Alas, I wasn't so lucky.

A few more minutes passed and again I asked, "Are we almost there?"

Again, my father said, "Just over the next hill, son."

This back-and-forth went on at least five more times and each time he told me, "Just over the next hill," compounding my confusion, until finally we were indeed approaching a hill. And the company picnic was terrible. I had been told we would be there "momentarily" a hundred times and when we actually did arrive, I went to the petting zoo and was spit on by a llama.

But when I think back on all the car trips I took with my parents, the "just over the next hill" stuff isn't what stands out to me. What I remember now, most likely only because I am now a parent, was the kids' complete lack of safety. The adults didn't wear seat belts, so we kids, always mimicking our parents, never bothered with them, either.

I had an Uncle Bob who in the late 1970s had a new Lincoln Town Car and if our seat belts weren't fastened, it would make a continuous beeping sound. But instead of minding the car's warning and buckling our safety belts, my uncle taught me to gently pull on the belt and let out a little slack so the beeping would stop.

Today you absolutely must have the safest car seats and seat belt systems. The government has stepped in and won't even let children face the front of the car until they are a certain age. This makes for some strange communication with my kid. He is facing the back and I am facing the front. In an effort to overcome this obstacle, a lot of parents hang a mirror on the backseat in front of the baby. Then when they drive, they tilt their own rearview mirror down and to the right so they can watch their baby slobber and coo. Who needs to see the road, when you and your baby could just sit there and stare at each other in four different dimensions?

My family always had station wagons. My parents had one, my grandparents had one, and a few of my aunts and uncles had them. The wagons had armrests that folded down between the driver and the passenger. I, being the youngest member of my family, and the only one who could actually fit my narrow behind onto this armrest, was "rewarded" as being the only child in the family who could sit there. Yikes! Nice place to put a kid. I couldn't even wear a seat belt in that "seat" if I wanted to. My throne was not a place the car manufacturers envisioned people sitting down. They were probably envisioning that other drivers would use the armrest for things like, well, arms. Not *my* family. That was J.J.'s seat and I would have screamed bloody murder if anyone ever had the audacity to try to take it from me. In hindsight, I think they were trying to kill me.

Jackie, having surpassed the sixty-pound milestone required by the state of California, has now graduated from the conventional baby seat to the booster car seat. This has proved to be so much easier for traveling and he loves it. I went to the store with him and showed him the long row of seats and let him pick his out. As he scanned the merchandise, I was hoping he wasn't going to pick the "My Little Pony" seat. And he didn't. He picked out a sporty-looking black and red booster and "helped" me assemble it in the parking lot. What a difference a seat makes. He went from looking like a helpless pansy baby to looking downright cool. His new seat had armrests and a bitchin' headrest so when he was in it, he looked like Robo-Cop. It even had little retractable cup holders on either side that are great for holding juice and I'm grateful to the manufacturer for sparing me from the all-too-common practice of having to pull over every time my kid drops his sippy cup and cries out, "Juice! Juice!" until I stop the car and retrieve it from under the seat. The retractable cup holders are also an excellent place to stash Matchbox cars and hide them for later.

I'm glad my kid no longer has to suffer through the indignity of a baby seat. What a production. Aside from it being a royal pain in the ass to transport from car to car, I always found it a little emasculating that to go for a ride around the block he had to be strapped in like a test pilot trying to break the land speed record. When I was growing up it wasn't uncommon to spend entire car trips on the driver's lap next to a six-pack of beer. Thankfully, I never sailed through a windshield. Car seats today are as difficult to figure out as diapers! Different seats for all weights, sizes, and shapes. Selfishly, I must admit that the best part of Jackie's new car seat is that he can get in and out of it himself. No longer do I have to risk tearing my abdominal wall hoisting a heavy, leg-kicking baby into Chuck Yeager's chair.

You will find as you navigate the first few years of your baby's life that there are many other advantages to being a parent, aside from just the HOV lane. For instance, if you have a baby and wait in line for a restroom, you are an idiot. Seriously. For God's sake, one of a baby's best attributes is its ability to inflict guilt on others. No one that stands in line for a bathroom can tell a three-year-old to take a hike. Especially if there are several other people around to witness the callousness. Many times I have rushed headlong into the front end of a bathroom line. The trick is to act boldly and with assurance. Don't pussyfoot your way toward the front of the line. Walk to the front of the line as if your daughter is about to vomit tuberculosis onto whoever dares to stand in your way. If you do this, you will almost always be the next one into the bathroom. If you find yourself behind some asshole who won't give up his place in line, give your baby a little pinch on her chubby thigh. If you do this just hard enough, the baby will start screaming and crying and then you can ask again and point to the hysterical baby as proof of your urgency. Practice the pinch at home a couple of times to figure out the right amount of force to use. You don't want to be out in public pinching your baby like some sick maniac.

I can remember many evenings that Nik and I were at California Pizza Kitchen when Jackie would tell us he had to go potty. This is great news if you also have to use the bathroom. A parent gets to saunter across the dining room with confidence. We know full well that when we get to the restrooms we will be able to use the men's *or the ladies'!* That's right, all you childless suckers. If you have a kid, the ladies part like the Red Sea to put you next in line for their sacred room. For those of you who have not yet experienced this, I urge you to get out there and do it. Did you know that some ladies' rooms have couches? What the hell is that about, gals? How long has this been going on? Maybe that's why girls always go to the bathroom in groups. *There's a couch!* If they put a couch in the men's room of the local sports bar, there would be as many guys in the bathroom as there would be at the bar! Also, women's bathrooms are fascinatingly clean. Frankly, I don't know how they do it. There is no writing on the mirror over the sink. There isn't even writing in the bathroom stalls. Women actually just sit and stare straight ahead when they take a dump. Impressive. You would think that out of sheer boredom some girl with a three-beer buzz would write "You suck!" on one of the walls, but she doesn't.

Women are mysterious. Every men's room has at least a few pages of dialogue on the stall walls. It is really staggering how the conversation keeps going between men who have never seen each other. One guy will write "You suck!" Underneath that, someone else will write "No, YOU suck!" A few months will go by and a separate man will add to the conversation "I'll suck both of you!" Then he will be gracious enough to add a phone number if anyone else wants to take him up on his services. Under that exchange, some genius will draw a diagram of what it would look like if the third guy did, indeed, hook up with the first two guys to show them how well he sucks. I'm guessing it's somewhere between cave drawings and the Pony Express in terms of effectiveness and expediency.

The women's bathroom, in complete contrast, is perfectly spotless. Women don't throw paper towels at the trash can; they place the towel inside. This means that there aren't paper towels lying in a mountain on the floor. Having used many ladies' rooms with Jackie, it seems that for some reason, women clean up after themselves even when no one is watching.

Being able to use the ladies' room is great but it isn't the absolute best bathroom a baby can buy. That title goes to the bathroom at places that claim they don't have a bathroom! We have all had the experience of walking into a gas station or a yogurt shop about to burst and asking the cashier for a key to the restroom. The cashier will look up with giant, fake-sorry eyes and say, "Sorry, we don't have one." Yes, you do. In fact, I am pretty sure it would be against the freaking law if you stood here making coffees for eight hours and they made you hold it in the whole time. I know you have a bathroom. You know I know you have a bathroom. Let me use the bathroom! They don't. I have tried every possible response to "We don't have a bathroom." I have even looked a woman in the eye and said, "Then where do you shit?" The only bathroom key you can bring to these places is your child. The assholes behind these "We don't have a bathroom" counters have no answer to a wandering two-year-old. Next time you have to take a whiz, aim your child behind the counter at the Coffee Bean. Just let him wander around for a few seconds between baristas. After a while, go behind the counter and act terrified like you thought you lost your child. When you pick your baby up, look at the barista and announce, "Bathroom!" Then just walk into the storeroom and pee in the sink. They won't stop you if you have the baby with you.

But restroom lines aren't the only lines you can jump if you are with a baby. If there are a couple of teenagers on the swings at the local park, they have to get up for you and your baby. If you and another car arrive at the same parking spot at the same time, point to the baby seat behind you and mouth "Baby" through the glass. Don't slow down. Keep the car rolling to-ward the spot as if you already know the person will give it up. You don't have to have your baby with you in order for this to work, by the way. If you are alone, when you get out of the car, point to the baby seat and really loudly say "Stay!" and then run into the store as fast as you can. If you see the parking spot person when you are in the store, just keep nervously looking out the window of the store toward your car. Ask the stranger,

"Did I leave my windows open?" At this point you will have two or three people shopping for you. Also, if you have your baby with you at the grocery store and don't want to wait in any lines, act like you can't handle it all and ask to go ahead. If someone looks like they aren't going to let you go ahead, say something quick like, "Oh my God, I think I might drop my baby!"

They'll move. (This works really well at the liquor store.)

Another benefit to being a parent is Happy Meals. McDonald's will serve you food in a cool, colorful box, with a handle on it and a toy inside. Until you're ten. As a society, I think this is where the wheels fall off. We need to give away more toys with dinner. Grown-ups would eat out a lot more often if we knew we could order a meal and get a toy with it. Look how excited we get about fortune cookies. Those fortunes haven't been updated in years but we all still act like morons when they are placed on the table with the check. My house is building up a nice burger toy collection. I don't want to throw any of them away. I know they seem like complete junk but if you wait just twenty years or so they will be awesome again.

For a reason unbeknownst to me, my in-laws never threw away any burger toys. Regardless of what the toy was or where it came from, it was put in a large plastic storage container. This went on throughout Nik and her brother's childhood. They are ten years apart, so whenever Jackie goes to his grandparents' house, he can open the lid to three decades of burger toys! It is awesome. There are cars that are half cookie. There is a rubber ruler that is wearing a graduation cap and holding a diploma that appears to be four inches long. There is the entire cast of the television show *Dinosaurs*. There is the Count from *Sesame Street* in a helicopter. There is a train with wolves painted on the side. There is a tiny bus with an ant driver and ant passengers. There are fruits and vegetables with faces. (And weapons!) There is even a mummy that can throw a tiny plastic basketball. Most people likely considered these toys junk no more than a few days after the Happy Meals were purchased. And perhaps they were right. However, if you save all of the burger toys you ever see and wait until you have grandchildren, you will become a god among men.

I mentioned earlier that children are incredible at inflicting guilt on other people. Conversely, kids also have a stupendous ability to absolve us of guilt. When you are a parent you can lie pretty much at will and use your baby as the main character in that lie. Instead of feeling guilty about lying, you actually begin to feel entitled to lie. How many times in your life have you been forced to sit through a lame barbecue or recital of some kind? During all of those instances, didn't you wish you could just look the host in the eye and tell them, "Sorry, I can't take it, I gotta get out of here." Well, when you have a baby, you *can!* It's fantastic. All you have to do to get out of hearing your grandma tell you the same story for the hundredth time is stand up with your baby and say, "Wow, she feels hot!" Then just walk away. Walk all the way to your car and drive home. For the rest of the afternoon, when people ask where you are, everyone will say sympathetic things like "He had to leave. His baby girl has a fever." The entire party will chime in "Aww, poor little girl!" And "He is such a great daddy."

Indeed I am. I know that I could be home playing My Little Pony instead of sitting here with you dopes.

This tactic is basically foolproof. No one will ever really suspect that you lied. Only a psychopath would use his child as an excuse to leave a party. Only someone who is truly evil would make up a story about his child being sick to get out of a barbecue early. Well, I am a truly evil psychopath. My son has gotten me out of more lame events than I can count. You can tell your friends, "I can't get a sitter." You don't even have to be that specific. You can be very vague and say something like "My son hasn't been acting like himself lately." No one really wants to get any deeper with that one. The only risk you run (aside from the obvious negative karma) is that your friends might stop by your house to see if your child is okay. You have to be prepared in case this happens. If you told everyone at the dance recital that your son hasn't been acting like himself lately and you should stay home, everyone better act the part when they come by. Start by taking a really long time to answer the door. Before you open it, make your hair stand straight up and act really sleepy. Then dress your son in your wife's blouse and tell him to answer the door in mommy's high heels. The kid will love it and your neighbor will leave quickly. If you have a daughter, answer the door holding a porn DVD. Tell your friend that you found it in your daughter's ViewMaster. Act like you have been crying. Then hand the DVD to your friend and ask him to get rid of it for you. Later, his wife will find it and then he'll have to do all the explaining. When the story gets back to you about your daughter having it in her ViewMaster, act appalled and then ask how your friend could stoop so low. Then tell everyone you know that you heard your friend is addicted to porn.

The next baby advantage is the mother lode. If you don't have kids, this next bit of information may influence you to make some immediately. When you have a child, you can fart whenever you want. The younger the child, the harder you can let it rip. Once your daughter reaches five years old, she can say things like "No, I didn't" and blow your cover. But when your baby cannot talk, you can literally fart everywhere, in front of anyone you want. It's like being the president. You can even fart in church. When the people sitting next to you have tears in their eyes and look in your direction, just look down at your baby and act embarrassed. Then leave mass early. This *always* works. Always. Just do your best to make your farts silent. Obviously you don't want to grind out a chain saw and blame it on the ten-pounder sitting on your wife's lap. That would be grotesque. If you can successfully eke out a couple of half-cheek sneaks, though, your baby is a great scapegoat.

You can also fart in restaurants and at parties. You can even try to make yourself fart while getting a speeding ticket. Maybe you can make the cop puke.

Having children definitely has its advantages. I have pointed out a bunch to you here in this chapter. One I have not mentioned yet is that when you have a child, you know what it is like to truly think of someone else before you think of yourself. If you have a baby you know that life is beyond precious. You know that you have an opportunity to give a little better than you got. All of the things that you think were missing from your own childhood, you can now overcompensate with this one. That is the true advantage to having children.

Plus, you never know when you'll need a kidney.

9

SUPERPOWERS

As your babies grow into toddlers, you will begin to notice that they are developing superpowers. However, they don't use them to fight evil like good, rational, normal people do. Children use their superpowers only for bad. A child uses his superpowers all day, every day, for the sole purpose of disrupting the flow of the home and the function of the parent.

One of the first superpowers your children will develop is the ability to turn their bodies into jelly and make them impossible to put down. I call this superpower "Baby with No Bones" and it is used primarily in crowded places like shopping malls and supermarkets when our kids do not want to be put down on the floor and you can't let go of their arms or they will fall and smash their faces on the ground. It's brilliant. On days when you have foolishly decided not to bring a stroller to the store, you quickly regret it when your baby decides to flex this skill. You will try to get your daughter to leave the mall or just walk in the general direction of another store when suddenly she turns into Baby with No Bones and physically transporting her becomes an impossibility. Her legs, arms, and torso fill up with a super heavy, bloblike jelly that makes her collapse to the floor like one of those nifty travel cups.

If you try to pick your kids up once they have become Baby with No Bones, it is too late. They become invertebrates and slide right through your arms and hands. We have all seen this happening to other parents out in public. It's pathetic. Grown men and women wrestling with a thirty-pound child like it's an alligator covered in bacon grease. If a child decides to go the Baby with No Bones routine, you are left with no choice but to wait out the storm. If you absolutely cannot do this, you might want to attempt to lay your son down on the mall floor lengthwise and then proceed to drag him out to the car by his feet. Warning: This action is usually followed by a visit from child services but sometimes you just have to get the hell home!

Invisibility is another popular superpower that little kids possess. This one will both surprise you and fill you with terror. Little-kid invisibility also tends to be reserved for large public places. Kids can whip out this superpower at a farmer's market, the mall, the airport, carnivals, and the beach. The same child who hangs on your legs all day and won't leave you alone for one second at an intimate gathering in the comfort of friends or family suddenly vanishes in a sea of hundreds. They don't give any clues as to when or why they might turn invisible, they just go *poof* and leave you standing in a state of utter panic.

All day long our kids make us watch what they are doing. Every single day, our children ask us: "What are you doing?" "Can I help?" All day long our kids ask us question after question about nothing until we wish they would disappear. Kids can sense when we feel this way and they store it away to use against us during the next trip to the beach.

After you have covered everyone in sunscreen, put down your blanket, handed a bucket and shovel to your son, then bent down to take off one of your shoes . . . it happens. You look up and he is gone. I don't mean "gone" like "Hey, this is weird, I wonder where that little rascal ran off to." I mean "gone" like jog-up-and-down-two-miles-of-beach-with-three-lifeguards-and-an-off-duty-cop-where-the-fuck-did-my-child-go gone. That is an example of your kid using his amazing powers of invisibility.

The same child who can't find a place to hide during hide-and-seek is the same child that you have to make announcements for over the loudspeaker at a baseball game. And really, I can't help but wonder why it is that children are incapable of finding and staying in a hiding place. It's ironic that hide-and-seek is a kid's game but kids are fucking terrible at it. If they hide under a bed, they leave a leg sticking out. If they hide in the closet, they sing aloud to themselves, without realizing that sound can travel through wood. If they hide in the garage, they knock over an entire shelf of tools and set off the car alarm. These same children who cannot physically make themselves still and quiet for a count of thirty seconds in their own bedroom will have you calling the local police to help find them in a count of two seconds out in public. I used to laugh when I saw little kids wearing crazy blue Mohawk wigs and fake dreadlocks at Dodgers games. Now I understand why. It's so their parents can find them in a fucking crowd. The next time I take Jackson to a game, I am going to make him paint his chest blue and wear a court jester's hat. No one is gonna lose sight of that guy. I think that's why you see so many umbrellas at the beach. It isn't really for shade. If we wanted shade, we wouldn't be at the beach. The reason there are so many umbrellas on the beach is so parents can have a landmark to show their children.

"The *yellow* umbrella. No, not *lellow*. The *yellow* umbrella that is *right there!*" My grandma used to make my father wear a bright red cowboy hat while he played in the wheat field behind their house. That way she could always see the top of his head from inside. I'm thinking of having Jackie's entire head dyed bright orange.

Whenever one of our kids uses their power of invisibility on us we assume they are long, long gone. We envision them in a bus traveling cross-country with a band of hippies or in some creep's van. We imagine them in a fishing boat being driven overseas for child slavery. They never are. The true magic power of invisibility is being able to use it in the closest of quarters. After we have had forty heart attacks and have enlisted the help of fifty strangers to form a makeshift dragnet, the kid is never very far away. That is the awesomeness of their invisibility. Our lost kid is usually about nine feet from where we saw her last. When we find her, she is very calm and has no idea what all the fuss is about. What's peculiar is when you get her home, shake sand out of her shoes, and a bus pass falls out.

Kids also have x-ray vision and bionic hearing. If you pick up a Reese's peanut butter cup and immediately put it behind your back, your child will race in from the other room and say, "Can I have one?" Kids can see right through our bodies and identify candy. It's a real doozie. They can also see through our bodies and identify when we are full of shit. If you try to explain to your son why he isn't going to the mall as promised, he will see right through you. I could lay out a detailed explanation about how I need to wait for a very important man to call the house so I can talk to him about buying a leopard and lots of gum. Jackson will look right in my eye and say, "We're not going to the mall because you want to watch the Jets game?" He's never wrong. He sees right through me with his x-ray vision.

The best is when kids can use their x-ray vision to see through bitchy strangers. One day Jackie and I were in line at the pharmacy when a lady came up to us and told us that she had been standing where we were in line but then ran to grab one more item. She said that the man in front of us (who was no longer there) was holding her spot. I was about to let the lady into the line, when Jackson said, "My dad and I have been waiting here at *least* five minutes and we never saw you. It wouldn't be fair if you got in front of us now." The old lady gave us a dirty look and dragged her sorry ass to the back of the line, where she belonged. This is one of the only times in my life I have ever seen a kid use his superpower for good, by the way.

Bionic hearing is one of the most annoying superpowers our kids have, though. If you open a newspaper, they will run to the kitchen table from the basement and say, "What are you doing? What are you reading? What is it, Daddy?" Whoa! Slow down, little man. It's a freaking paper, not SpongeBob spy gear.

Kids are the absolute best at detecting when their parents are about to have sex. If I even look at Nik suggestively and she gives me a sexy smile in return, Jackie will burst through the door to look under the bed for lost Lincoln Logs. Sex detection is one of the most time-honored traditions passed down through the generations. Spouses the world over have become experts at perfectly silent sex. Even if you are under the blankets with the door locked and the television on high volume, your kid can burst into the room like a freaking ninja.

There was one night that I swear I thought Jackson slid under the door as a liquid, and then regrouped into a solid once inside. Luckily, Nik and I were still clothed and didn't have any explaining to do. I'm sure that many of you have had no such luck. How many times have you told your kid that you and your wife were wrestling? How many times have you told your kid that you hurt your foot and Mommy was just carrying you on her back across the bed? How many of you have had to explain that Daddy was on fire and Mommy had to put him out with her bottom?

It happens. It doesn't make you a bad person. Your kids will become so exceptional at hearing you thinking about having sex that eventually you will give up anyway. You and your wife both know that the next time you are having sex is when your kid goes to Grandma's for the weekend.

As kids get older, their bionic hearing gets better. However, the good news is that it lasts only for a limited time. Once they are teenagers they can't hear a fucking thing you say.

My kid can also fly. It is incredible to watch him sail through the air. The only problem is that he never seems to do it on purpose. Kids can fly at very strange times and from some strange angles. I once watched Jackson fall *up* a flight of stairs. Your son will jog around the roof of the house and climb down from the gutter with ease but if you blink while he is standing up in a shopping cart, he will fly. Kids stay airborne for odd amounts of time, too. I once watched Jackson fall off his bike while Nik and I were eating dinner. Somewhere between my first bite of salad and my coffee, I looked out the bay windows and Jackson fell off his bike and onto the driveway. It's not until I sat down to write this that I remembered that even more remarkably, the bike wasn't even moving!

When I was a kid, we fell off our bikes because we were riding too fast, like maniacs. We wiped out hard and fast. I don't have any memories of falling off of my bike—fully padded and helmeted—while still standing in the driveway! It took so long for Jackie to hit the ground one time that he just sort of looked around while in the air. But that example isn't a very good example of flying. It's more an example of flopping. Flopping isn't a superpower. Flopping is a way to tell the future. When your son continually flops around, like mine does, you know he isn't going to college on an athletic scholarship.

10

SAFE IS A FOUR-LETTER WORD

Why do our kids think we are so damn interesting? One day, and I don't know when it was, children stopped being able to play without adult supervision. I am not talking about leaving your child alone for some quiet time. I am talking about our children's utter inability to play by themselves. When I was a kid, grown-ups were really only around at dinner and to drive us to school. Moms and dads didn't sit next to you on the swings at the park. Parents didn't chase us through the woods with our friends. Mom and Dad didn't really know what the inside of the neighbor's house looked like, either. That is because when I was a kid we wanted to be left alone with other kids. We didn't want our parents watching us play army or football or touching each other's cranks.

Sometime over the last thirty years or so, the focus of playtime has shifted. What used to be two or more kids paying attention to only each other has changed into our one kid constantly saying "Look at me!" Our kids don't let *us* out of *their* sight. When I was a kid, if you saw a dad or mom rolling around on the ground with a kid at the park, they were in mid-brawl. Whenever you were at a friend's house and a parent showed up, your first thought was, I hope I'm not in trouble. Almost never do you see just three kids playing by themselves anymore. Kids need constant attention and positive affirmation. It's annoying. I get it. You can hop on one leg. Wow. You are the best.

When I was a kid, I would get on my bike and ride over to my friend's house and come home around five, in time for dinner. These days, your daughter will show you how cool she looks getting on the bike for the first forty-five minutes. Then there will be a half hour of talk about how cool the new helmet looks on her head. The next hour will be spent in your driveway as your kid shows you every "trick" she knows on her bike. I should point out to you what you already know. These tricks suck. Our children are simply horrible at tricks. Did the definition of the word *trick* change and I missed the memo? A "trick" to our children is just a "thing" to us. Jackie will ask me to watch his supercool new trick and he will stand on one leg and hop up and down once. Then there is an awkward pause because I think he is breaking my balls and the real trick hasn't started yet. Eventually I will have to say "That was awesome, pal!" to not hurt his feelings. That's another thing that I find a bit annoying about parenthood. Kids have a lot more feelings than they used to. Our parents would tell us we were morons to our faces and it wouldn't bother us. These days, if you don't applaud your child's Lego creation long enough, everyone has to talk about it in family therapy. In short, kids today are complete pussies.

What happened to all the tough kids who would walk into the forest and build themselves a fort? Today you walk with your daughter through Target and buy her a shiny plastic fort to be set up in the backyard. Your child will be in her shiny plastic fort for just a few seconds before she starts yelling, "Daddy! Look, I'm as tall as the door! I'm as tall as the door!" And like dolts, we parents will wave from the porch and shout some inane positive feedback like "Way to go, darling! You *are* as tall as the door!" And with that sentence, our children get weaker. What ever happened to forts made out of branches and sticks and old refrigerators? When I was a kid we would break bottles on rocks and spread the shards of glass around the outside of the fort for protection in case we were attacked. We never knew who might attack us but damnit, if they had bare feet they were going to go home bloody! When we were kids we didn't want to share our playtime with the adults. If one of our parents mentioned that they knew where our fort was, it would immediately be destroyed. In fact, half the fun of building a fort was knowing that in a couple of weeks you were going to tear it down. Today tearing down forts is taboo. It is also against all conceivable laws and rules to throw anything that was ever touched by your child into the trash.

Jackie is seven years old and we still have a Thomas the Tank Engine table in the garage with every train car accessory. Our guy hasn't gone near this table in at least three years but if I ask him if I can give it to Goodwill, he starts to hyperventilate. So it just sits there next to all of the Webkinz and Backyardigans dolls and the Oswald the Octopus beanbag game. I know not to touch any of it. The poor guy will have a heart attack.

It seems my son will have a heart attack if I am not watching pretty much everything he does during every waking moment. He is not unique on this one. Every kid I know these days is always clamoring out for attention and yelling "Come chase us!" Someone needs to tell these kids to kiss my ass and go chase themselves! When did this obsession with being chased start? "Come play with us!" Come watch us play catch!" "Come watch me play Wii!" This is acceptable and even cute for the first few years of your child's life. But after a while it becomes unbearable.

As a parent, I simply cannot figure out why our children find us so interesting. Why do they need us to watch them do every little thing? Why must our kids demand our attention when they are performing the most mundane tasks? The answer is simple. Everyone else in the world sucks. Kids their own age will tell them they are hopping on their leg the wrong way. Older kids will tease them for not climbing fast enough. Other grown-ups will simply ignore them. When our kids ask us to watch them, we watch them. When they are done doing whatever it is they were doing, we tell them how absofuckinglutely fantastic they are.

Who wouldn't go back to that well as often as possible? Hell, I would. Hell, I do! I'm a comic. Every night I walk onstage and for an hour I ask people to look at what I am doing. Then I ask them to watch again. I ask the audience to pay attention to me and only me for over an hour. Nik has been a working actress since she was nine! We all get into the business for the same reason: We want to be watched and told we are great. The difference between children and actors, of course, is that actors are usually told that they suck. So it would be a bit hypocritical of me to have a problem with our kids' constant need for attention. But I do, nevertheless. It bugs me. I think a lot of what our kids carve time out of our day to show us really sucks. What my kid shows me sucks and what your kid shows you sucks.

I was recently in the supermarket with Jackie and as I frantically looked over my shopping list, he said, "Daddy, look at this. You won't believe this!" I looked over at him and I can honestly tell you, dear reader, I had no idea what I was looking at. He was just standing there. Then he let out a big exhale and told me he had just beaten his old world record. I had to explain to my boy that I had no freaking idea what he was talking about. He explained to me like I was the special boy in class: "Standing on my tippy toes. I just broke my world record of standing on my tippy toes." Oh. Spectacular. Here, let me buy you some Animal Crackers.

I'm not really sure why children of this generation have an insatiable need to be watched. But I do know we have to watch them. If we don't watch our children every time they ask us, pretty soon they will just stop asking. Then depression will set in, years and years will go by, and you will be asking your children to watch you. You will need them to wipe your ass and help you in and out of cars. You will say "Watch me!" as you take your first steps with your new walker. You won't ask them to chase you through the woods but you will ask them to tell you about when you chased them through the woods. Because you will not be able to fathom how damn fast it all went by. Make sure, no matter how annoying it is, that your kids' "Watch me!" is usually met with an "I'm coming." Even if what they are doing sucks.

The only real way to get your kid to stop paying attention to you is to plop him in front of the television. Once you've done that, you can transform into a space alien made of ice cream and he still won't acknowledge your existence except to crane his neck because you make a better door than a window in front of the mesmerizing gay purple dinosaur.

Nik and I decided early on in Jackson's life that television was to be watched sparingly. We didn't think that television would really be any good for our guy. He should be out playing in the sun instead of staring at Teletubbies. Many other parents feel the same way as we do. The trick to taking this hard anti-television stance is standing your ground, especially when your kid is acting like a hyperactive whack job and you are sleep deprived. It's a little irresistible when you realize that one hour of

The Backyardigans would keep your kid perfectly still while you take a forty-five-minute nap on the couch next to him. There are some Saturdays when I thank the good Lord above that there is a *Phineas and Ferb* marathon on that starts at noon. That usually means that Daddy will get an hour nap and then be able to go upstairs and fix his fantasy football roster.

When I was a kid, I was allowed to watch TV for hours. And by hours, I mean consecutive hours and *hours*. Some days after school I would watch TV from three in the afternoon until ten at night. The only break was for dinner. Dinner in my house was at 6 P.M. sharp every night. No exceptions. Nowadays the best way to get Jackie to come sit at the table is to tell him that if he hurries he'll be able to watch TV while he eats. This is a double-edged sword. We are able to lure him to the table with television but once he is seated his brain turns to mush. He stares at the TV like a zombie. He rarely laughs. He just sits there perfectly still and stares and doesn't even blink. When my son watches TV during dinner he will forget to chew. It is one of the more interesting things to watch. He will take a big bite of macaroni and cheese and then look up at the television and just freeze. I'll watch him for a minute and say "Chew!" Then he will start chewing quickly to make up for the lag in action.

Kids do strange stuff like this all the time. Their sense of space and time are completely screwed up. Kids forget to brush their teeth for three days. On the fourth day, they will then brush their teeth for ten straight minutes, their little theory being that if they brush their teeth for ten minutes, it will undo the three days of neglect. This theory gets put into practice a lot with hand washing. If kids think their hands are particularly dirty, they will wash them for eternity. They will pump seven or eight helpings of Johnson & Johnson into their hands and start rubbing like OCD maniacs. Then they'll rinse and re-pump eight more times. If you try to explain to your son that washing his hands once, correctly, the first time will do the trick, he will then look at you like you are a person of little or no intellect. He will say, "I washed them five times so now they're really REALLY clean." Then you remember how tired you are and just say he is right and no pair of cleaner hands has ever existed.

I have also noticed that when you tell children to listen carefully, they make their eyes wider. Try this on your daughter right now. Don't ask her to listen. *Tell* her to listen. Get right in her face and say, "I really need you to listen. *Listen.*" She will make her eyes as big as saucers. Apparently kids do a lot of listening with their eyes. Maybe I should try helping Jackie chew through his ears.

The question remains, how much TV should we let our kids watch? Obviously, every kid is different. If your five-year-old daughter likes to unwind while watching the British Parliament sessions on C-SPAN, by all means, give her a pass. But if your son is just watching hours of guys getting kicked in the nuts over and over again on *When Animals Attack,* for the love of God, turn off the box. Then TiVo it. Then, after he is asleep, get super high on medical marijuana, watch it by yourself, and laugh until you piss in your adult diaper.

How much time should be spent playing video games is also a constant struggle. I want Jackie to be outside with his buddies, running in the backyard and surfing and swimming in the ocean. Instead, on many days, they are all on the Wii, surfing and swimming in my living room. Sometimes I'll tell Jackie that he has to play outside and that his video game time is over. I tell him no more video games today. Once he is outside, I kick everyone's ass on Mario Kart.

I am coming to the conclusion that this generation of parents is more hypocritical than our parents'. When our parents told us, "We didn't have this when we were kids," they meant it. Some of them didn't even have television. How can I tell my kid not to play too many video games? If Jackie had a time machine, I would have no credibility at all. I spent a good year playing Mike Tyson's Punch-Out. A year. Hell, I just finished one of the Twisted Metal games one week when he was at camp. That is all I did. I woke up and played Twisted Metal and Mike Tyson's Punch-Out. If I had to leave or use the restroom, I would pause the game and resume later. I can honestly say that in my early twenties there were actual years that went by that I never used my TV for anything but Mortal Kombat. So I try to go easy on the little guy when it comes to TV and video games. He gets to blow off steam and watch it for a couple of hours in a row each week. As far as the video games go, I am not hooking the Wii back up until I am absolutely positive he will never again beat me at Mario Kart.

But maybe we parents of this new generation are overthinking everything. Perhaps the television *is* just a godsend of a distraction and not frying my child's brain. Perhaps if my kid cries all night until *I'm* ready to wake up (at 11 A.M.), he won't have abandonment issues into adulthood and turn into a pedophile or cannibal. Perhaps if I don't baby-proof my house, my kid will learn to take it like a man.

Fuck cabinet locks and crib bumpers. Let's strip our homes of outlet plugs, helmets, and water wings (why are those so hard to put on my kid's little arms anyway?). George Carlin once had a routine explaining that children should be pitted against one another in a great, grand plan of survival of the fittest. It was hilarious but in a way I agree with him. The only flaw in the logic is that if we let our kids hash it out among themselves without our safety precautions, only the big bullies will survive. It seems there should be some type of safety mechanism in place to ensure that a few nerds get through high school and college without dying. Many games we used to play as children are now banned in the school systems. Remember dodgeball? Remember the rules to dodgeball? If you were fat or wore glasses, you didn't show up to school that day because you would die.

Every dodgeball game started the same way. The gym teacher would hand out a few volleyballs and you had one mission on your mind. Pick out the weakest member of the herd and kill him.

Exchange student? Dead! Fat kid with asthma? Dead! Popular kid not paying attention and looking in the wrong direction? KILL HIM. That was how it went when we were kids. We found people weaker than we were and tried to eliminate them. Sometimes we were successful and sometimes it backfired. Every once in a while you would throw the ball as hard as you could at an unsuspecting fatso and by complete chance and luck, he would catch it. This was a nightmare situation. You watched it unfold in slow motion since the kid didn't really catch the ball so much as he cradled it into the folds of his fat. Regardless, when someone catches the dodgeball, whoever threw it is out. Now you have been eliminated and the fat, asthma-riddled exchange student gets to roam the great plains of New Jersey for at least another day. What's striking is that this barbaric "game" all took place under the watchful eye of adult supervision. It happened at our school! A teacher handed us a ball and instructed us to throw it at other students.

We have really pussified our country lately. No such games are allowed anymore. In some schools they are trying to eliminate tag. Tag! You know tag, the game where you win by simply touching someone else and saying the words "You're it!" After tag gets eliminated, what games will be left to play? What games have zero contact and can ensure that no one's feelings will be hurt? Maybe in the next decade kids will all assemble in the gymnasium and play Clue, Chutes and Ladders, and Candy Land for PE. You can laugh but we aren't that far away from this being a reality. When I was a kid, it didn't matter what game the gym teacher had set up for us. No matter what it was we would find a way to make it as violent as possible. I can remember playing kickball in fifth-grade PE and a few of the students convinced the coach that he should allow "peg outs." Peg outs were basically that when a kid was running the bases, you could "peg" him with the ball. We argued to the gym teacher that we couldn't possibly throw a kickball to a base because it was too big and awkward. To keep the game fair, we should be able to get the runner out by hitting him or her with the ball as they ran. The teacher actually bought this logic and for the next seven years of my life, I tried to decapitate any boy or girl on the basepaths. I also knew full well that if I was running between second and third, then others were trying to kill me. These were good times. Not only were these good times but they taught me skills that I still use today in the real world. I can duck very quickly. I seem to have a sixth sense about things flying toward my head. I am very difficult to sneak up on, too. I can directly attribute all of these life skills to years of trying to survive a simple game of schoolyard kickball.

These days, every parent wants to wrap their kids in bubble wrap. Safety is an obvious concern for all parents but I think sometimes we all go a bit overboard. When I was a kid, I never owned a helmet for my bike. I never wore kneepads or elbow pads. If one of the neighborhood kids saw me wearing a helmet, the ass-kicking would begin immediately. It wasn't that our parents weren't concerned for our safety. They were. The problem was that we kids had zero regard for our own safety. When I was about ten years old, my friends and I would climb up the trellis onto the roof of my family's garage and box with puffy ski mittens for gloves. The rules were simple. No hitting each other in the face and when you fell off the garage, you lost. Can you imagine what would happen if you even saw your kid climbing up the wall of the garage? You would yank him down by his waistband and throw him into therapy. Now imagine six or seven kids, all in a group, on the roof of your garage, throwing relentless body punches and laughing. I am guessing you would call the police. Hell, I would. I would dial 911 and simply tell the operator, "Come get these kids off my garage!" Unless Jackie was winning.

When we were kids, we would helmetlessly ride our bikes into other towns and pick fights with other kids playing on their front lawns. And lose. After we got the snot beat out of us we would ride our bikes home. I distinctly remember calling my mother from Montville, New Jersey, (nine miles from Verona) and telling her I probably wasn't going to make it home in time for dinner. She then thanked me for calling and hung up. To get to Montville from Verona you have to ride on Route 46 for about a mile. That is a freeway that truckers use to get from rural New Jersey to Manhattan. I had a little crew of twenty eleven-year-olds weaving our bikes between trucks and cars as they whizzed by our pant legs at seventy miles an hour. We truly had no regard for our own personal safety. But oddly, we never got hurt, either. I remember one kid on my street, Danny Peterson, got a concussion. He didn't get it by flying off a garage or getting hit by a car, though. Danny ran down the hallway in his house with socks on and slipped. He hit his head on the hallway wall and had to be rushed to the hospital. Pussy.

The garage was a sort of testing ground for all types of new dangerous activities. I remember a bunch of us climbed up on top of Jeff Sontag's garage with plastic garbage bags. One by one, we all jumped off the garage with the garbage bags over our heads, hoping they would work like a parachute. They didn't. The first kid off the garage roof landed with a sickening thud. We never thought that the same thing would happen to the next five kids off the roof; we just thought that the first kid must not have done it right. One after another we jumped off the garage roof and one after another we landed and thought the other had died. We were all bent up in unnatural positions and we all had the wind knocked out of us. As we lay there in a pile holding thirty-gallon garbage bags, we began trying to suffocate each other. Goddamn, that was fun.

When I was a kid we also would have rock fights. Rock fights are exactly what they sound like. You grab a handful of rocks and throw them at your friends, hoping to hurt them. Whoever doesn't wind up with stitches or missing teeth wins. We also would have stick fights, skateboard fights, chewed food fights, and firewood fights. All of these games involve trying to maim your opponent with the weapon of choice. It takes a very special skill set to have a sword fight with a skateboard.

Jackie has a pair of light sabers in the garage. They are standard issue, *Star Wars* replica plastic light sabers. Whenever he asks me to play light sabers with him I have to lay out some ground rules. I tell him that we have to be careful not to hit each other too hard or on the hands. We then go out into the front yard and have a very gentle sword fight with our light sabers. I think back to my own childhood games and wonder what the hell happened to me. I wonder when I got so soft. I used to throw rocks at my best friend and here I am trying to teach my son the gentle way to have a *fake* sword fight. Sometimes Jackie and I never even get to the actual sword fight. Jackie will spend a good twenty minutes deciding which light saber he wants to use. He will contemplate the merits of using the orange versus the blue light saber. We will really break this down for a while, trying to get to the bottom of which light saber is best for each of us. This is something that used to make me crazy but after patience rang my doorbell I have come to love it. As a dad, it is important to realize that sometimes setting up the ground rules *is* the actual game. Jackie and I have spent hours talking about which Legos will be best for our upcoming space-ship battle. As a parent, don't be in such a hurry to get the game started. The real fun is happening right in front of you. Listen to the bizarre reasoning that your kid will give in choosing a par-ticular Lego. One day the game will happen. Until then I am more than happy to let my son unravel a good half hour of ground rules.

As parents today we are hyperaware of perverts roaming our streets. These predators are constantly prowling around waiting to swoop in and steal our children. We take many precautions so our children will never fall prey to these savage animals. We confirm and reconfirm pickup times. We watch our kids walk into the doors of the school. Many times, we even remove children's names from their clothing so a stranger can't call them by name.

Needless to say, I support all of these precautions. It just stuns me how little we cared about these predators when I was a child. In every neighborhood there are always one or two houses about which as a kid you are told "A pervert lives there." My friends and I would always respond in the same way: "Awesome!" Whether these were urban myths or if indeed a sex offender lived at the given address was of little or no consequence. We wanted action. We liked to be chased and we liked to fight and we liked to look danger in the face. I remember being told that there was a sex offender living in a house behind the middle school. My friends and I rang his doorbell the day before Halloween and yelled out, "Trick or treat!" When he answered the door we didn't have any costumes on and when the man asked us what we were dressed as we told him we were dressed as students on the day before Halloween. The man told us to wait while he looked for some candy to give us. We were all very pissed off that the guy didn't invite any of us inside.

The rumor at my middle school growing up was that there was a pair of janitor brothers who raped kids and then had sex with each other. As a result of this information we all signed up for janitor duty at the school and hoped to be paired with the suspected brothers. I should point out that none of us wanted to be raped by the janitors behind the middle school. We did, however, want to see if the things we were being told were true. We wanted something, anything, to happen to break up the monotony of day-to-day suburban life in Verona, New Jersey.

I can vividly remember when on one of our bicycle excursions to Montville, my friends and I passed a man parked at a Dunkin' Donuts. The man saw the group of us preteens coming and pulled over. By the time we arrived at the man's car we could see that his pants were pulled down to his knees and he was violently beating off.

We circled the masturbator's car with our bikes. We pounded on the hood of his car with our hands. We yelled at him to beat off faster and harder. We were fucking insane! The man drove off. We then followed him for freaking miles. Every time the guy had to stop at a red light, we would again circle his car and bang on his hood yelling for him to start jerking off again. When the light turned green, he couldn't pull away without running one of us over. Other cars would be stuck in the little-boy-bike-gang traffic jam. We would bang on those cars and yell, "That guy is jerking off!" The other cars would then honk their horns and pandemonium ensued.

Eventually, when the traffic was completely stopped at a light, we did the next logical thing. We pulled our pants down and mooned the perv. Thinking back now, I remember way too many instances when kids had their pants down in public. My parents would pull my pants down in public to spank my bare ass in front of the neighbors. We would moon passing cars because we were bored. We would hide behind trees and wait for high school senior girls to walk by and when they arrived we would pop out and grab their boobs and run away. What a difference a generation makes.

Nik and I have taught our guy that if he is ever unsure of a situation, to get the hell out. We have drilled into his head that he will never be wrong if he errs on the side of caution. I cannot imagine how I would react if my kid behaved the way I did as a kid in awkward situations. Imagine your son riding his bike in the middle of a busy street with no helmet on. Now imagine a guy in a car jerking off next to your child. Now picture your boy holding up traffic so he can pull his pants down and show the creep his eleven-year-old ass. There are so many things wrong with the way we behaved as children. It is a bit of a miracle that we are alive. If Jackie knew what a complete hyperactive mental patient I was as a kid, he would laugh at every bit of instruction I give him. Fortunately, by the time he reads this book, my hypnosis and Jedi mind tricks will have already taken a firm hold in his brain. If he reads this book and questions my authority I will tell him this is a work of fiction and the publishers made a terrible mistake in labeling it otherwise. Then he will ask me what fiction is and I will have successfully Jedi-mind-tricked him off the subject (which reminds me of another great thing about having kids—you always have someone around you can bullshit and fool with petty lies).

11

PLAY BALL

I don't think I'm the only father out there who wants his son to be a professional athlete. The moment Jackie was born, I started predicting what his grown-up height and weight would be and what position he would play and in what sport. As I looked down at the three-pound premature baby lying in an incubator, I declared with proud certainty that he would be "six four, two-twenty." I don't think I was that far off. At the age of six, Jackie was a few inches over four feet and growing at an exhausting rate of about half an inch per month. I think I pushed my luck, though, when I also exclaimed, "He'll be a wide receiver *and* a centerfielder!" Obviously, showing such ballsy bravado is a risk when your child is in an incubator. It would be a lot easier if we dads all waited until our children were roaming the football

157

field on a Saturday and then yelled from the stands, "My son is going to be a linebacker!" But, like most gambles, the higher the risk, the higher the reward. So, as my son lay in his little space tube in the hospital, having been out of the womb for less than twenty-four hours, I told anyone within earshot that my son was going to be a wide receiver *and* a centerfielder.

To make sure my prediction would come true, I would practice tackling my toddler as he stumbled around the house. As I took swipes at his legs I would shout, "Keep your feet!" and other things I imagined his future college coach would yell to him. I would routinely hand Jackie a tiny football and shout, "Hut, hut, hike!" and smother his little body down onto the couch cushions. I really was convinced that I was molding a world-class NFL stud. My little Jackie boy was well on his way to being the number-one wide receiver for the 49ers. How could he not? He had his father teaching him how to keep his feet and tackling him into couch pillows. I knew what I was doing. Even though I never played a down of organized football in my life, I knew I was raising a Hall of Famer. I was wrong.

Jackie's first experience with organized sports was a soccer league on the west side of Los Angeles that I signed him up for. The games for the league were on a field that was very close to our house and Nik and I thought it would be a great way for Jackie to get some exercise with the other neighborhood kids. The entire process was charming and adorable. The name of the four-year-olds' soccer league was "Itty Bitty Soccer." We went to the local YMCA and picked up his uniform. We bought a great pair of cleats, shin pads, and wristbands. We made sure that regardless of skill, he would be the coolest-looking guy on the field. His jersey read number 10 and I spent the entire ride home explaining why 10 was the best number to have. (He wanted number 4 because he was four years old.) I told him how if something was the absolute best, grown-ups would say that it is a 10. So, if you wear the number 10, all the grown-ups will think you are the best kid on the field. He wasn't buying any of it.

Eventually, Nik said, "You love the show *Ben 10,* right?"

The little guy flipped out. *"Yes!* I want to be number ten like *Ben 10!"*

Problem solved. Thank you, wife.

When we got to the field on a foggy Saturday morning there was such hope in the air. Here we were at our son's first sporting event. Maybe he would take to it like a fish to water and run around and score goals all day! Maybe he would have to be put in the league with the six-year-olds because his dominance wasn't fair to others. Or maybe he would hate it because once the referee blew his whistle, this simple game of soccer became a blood sport. And hate it he did. To be honest, I didn't blame him. I was a little horrified by what I witnessed on that Saturday morning. I still am not sure who behaved worse—the children or the grown-ups, who were screaming at the top of their lungs at their kids. The previously civilized people who brought picnic baskets and lawn chairs to the soccer game were now werewolves. Lawn chairs were thrown on their sides and food flew out of parents' mouths as they screamed instructions to their four-year-olds.

I was appalled. I thought people acted this way only in the Valley. I thought this is why we moved—so we could have civilized soccer games on foggy Saturdays, blocks from the ocean. Parents now moved onto the field to yell at the referee. Millionaires were screaming at a volunteer ref and calling him a cocksucker. Obviously there were normal parents who used the soccer game as a social event to have deep, meaningful conversation without ever looking up at the field. Even I fought the urge to scream out to Jackie "Keep your feet!" (He could have used it.) My son, like most of the children on the field, was getting mauled. It dawned on me that lovely fall morning that if you are going to field a soccer team, you should probably at some point teach the kids how to actually play soccer. From the moment the game started, all the children blindly threw their bodies toward the ball and kicked as hard as they could. No one really seemed to care if they actually made contact with the ball. As long as there was some type of resistance on the other side of their little feet, they thought they were doing a fine job. They were savages. It looked like *Lord of the Flies* in cleats! Every time a pile of kids were separated, I expected to see someone holding a pig's head on a stick. There was no head on a stick but what I saw repeatedly was four-year-olds crying and running toward the sidelines to safety. No one (including myself) had the forethought to teach any of these kids how to pass and how to position themselves on a field. No one taught these Itty Bitty soccer players that it is against the rules to shove each other to the ground. No one taught these angels that once you are shoved to the ground, your parent is not allowed to run onto the field to pick a fight with the four-year-old who shoved you. No such education took place prior to the game and absolute bedlam was the result. They should have painted these kids' faces blue and called it Braveheart instead of soccer. Child after child climbed out from under a pile bleeding and crying and the parents would give the wounded player a juice box and a hug and usher them back on the field as quickly as possible. It was unbelievable.

As in most sports, there is always one kid who can literally run circles around everyone else his age. This day was no exception. On the opposing team was a curly-headed blond boy who could make magic with a soccer ball and his feet. Perhaps most strange was that this soccer savant was definitely the smallest kid out there by a good six inches. It didn't matter. The tiny, curly-headed kid was unstoppable. At halftime this kid had four goals. The rest of his team, as well Jackie's entire team, had zero. So at halftime the score was curly-headed Owen Meaney midget kid, 4, everyone else, 0. As Jackie sat next to Nik and me at the break, he started dropping little hints that maybe soccer wasn't for him. For example, "This is awful" and "I think my legs are broken." If I didn't know that the heart of a champion beat strongly inside my son's chest, I would have thought he didn't like it.

When halftime was over, it was more of the same. All the kids who had gotten kicked in the shins and thighs in the first half seemed now to just be roaming the field looking for someone to kick as payback. Piles of spastic kids followed the rolling soccer ball around the field and when they got within fifteen feet of it they began kicking wildly. Every once in a while the ball would roll out of bounds and under the lawn chairs of the maniacs. A mom or a dad would pick the ball up off the ground and absentmindedly throw it back onto the field and continue their discussion. That's when I had an epiphany. None of the warriors out on the field knew whose father I was and they didn't know what team I wanted to win. I made sure to track the ball so I would be the parent who got to throw it back on the field the next time it rolled out of bounds. Eventually a ball rolled off the field and I jogged over to scoop it up. First I looked at where Jackie was standing at midfield and I mouthed, "Don't move." Next I made a super overdramatic motion for all of the psycho-children to get ready for me to roll the ball over toward the goal. Then as they all began to run (sometimes kids are such dopes), I turned my body 180 degrees and rolled a perfect pass thirty feet ahead of Jackie toward the opposite goal. He was late in getting to the ball because he was still obeying my "don't move." He didn't realize that "don't move" only counts until your cheater father rolls you the perfect pass. Eventually Jackie caught up with the ball and sort of touched it with his foot. The ball went in the goal and I went nuts. I jumped up and down and fought the urge to yell "In your face!" to all of the wine-drinking parents around me.

If I am to be totally honest, I think the ball may not have ever touched my son's foot. I may have simply rolled a soccer ball past a four-year-old goalie. But I didn't care. My child tasted victory. More important, I tasted victory. I drove home a winner! During the drive, Jackie looked like a returning Vietnam War veteran. He had cuts and bruises all over him and he didn't want to talk about his day. He didn't really care about "his" goal. He just wanted to get home and get back to his normal life of Legos and books. At one point Jackie announced that he didn't want to play soccer anymore. I was heartbroken. I told him that he wasn't allowed to quit a sport every time his team lost or whenever the game got tough. I pointed out that he scored his team's only goal and that for him the day was a success. He didn't care. He thought soccer sucked and he was right. I made an agreement with him. I told him that he could quit soccer under one condition: He would give it at least one more chance and he would never quit karate. He agreed.

The next soccer game was worse than the first. There were three other soccer games on adjacent fields. If a ball from one field rolled onto another field, you now had four teams of hooligans kicking it. None of the kids could figure out where the out-of-bounds lines were. They all kept kicking the ball farther and farther away from the field. They completely ignored the referee's whistles and the shouts of their parents. They just kept running and kicking and falling and running and kicking until someone kicked a ball into a goal three fields away. No one noticed and no one cared. I now knew the exact definition of "mob mentality." If someone had told these kids to turn and murder someone, they all would have done it. It was freaking brutal. I had convinced myself that this week's soccer game would be more civilized. Where the other game was at a nondescript field, this game was going to take place on the field of a fancy private school. A Christian private school. I was relieved going in that the next time these kids were blindly kicking things it would be on a field with the word *Christian* in the title.

Apparently four-year-olds can really hold a grudge. Every kid who had gotten beat up in the first game was running across the separate fields to find the kid who had kicked them. When they spotted their target, they would sucker-kick the kid in the leg and run back onto the field where they were "playing." There was no play happening out on that battlefield. It was full-on war. Jackie was giving it his best try but I could see he was completely freaked-out by the bloodlust of the other players. His team won but he didn't score. (Neither did I.)

"What's the point of running around and getting kicked if I don't score any goals?" he asked. I tried to explain to him that his team had won. Even though he didn't score, his team scored more goals than the other team and they won the game. I told him that sometimes you score and your team loses and sometimes you don't score and your team wins. "I like it better when I score and my team loses."

I convinced Jackson to give soccer a third chance. I gave him the ol' "three times is the charm." I reasoned with him that maybe this time he would score a goal *and* his team would win. Maybe he would even score the winning goal. He agreed to go to one more game before he would decide whether to quit. Neither Nik nor I was able to attend the third game. We each had some stupid work thing that we couldn't get out of. Fortunately, one of our neighbors took Jackie to the game with their son and said they would watch both boys until we returned from work. It was perfect. Jackie's potentially final game wouldn't have me yelling at him to keep his feet. He wouldn't have his creepy father rolling perfect cheating passes his way. The entire game would unfold without me giving him any pointers. He would be out there in the real world fighting for himself and making up his own mind. That was the game in which my son got a head injury.

My cell phone vibrated in my pocket. My neighbor explained that a little girl and Jackie collided midfield and he got knocked out a little.

"What do you mean 'a little'?"

My neighbor explained that after the two kids collided, Jackson went stiff and gave a little shake. I asked what hospital they were at and she told me they weren't; there was a doctor at the field and he had declared that both kids were okay. Oh. We rushed home as quickly as we could and Jackson was acting completely normal. He wasn't out of it or slurring his words. Interestingly, when we asked him what happened, the little girl he ran into was replaced by "an older kid." We spent the rest of the day watching him and decided that the collision didn't cause a concussion or worse, brain damage. I spent the next four years wondering if we had misdiagnosed him.

Over the years, I have tried to get Jackie interested in other team sports besides soccer. After the whole soccer-for-psychos experiment my credibility wasn't what I had hoped. He had already been taking karate for two years and he loved it. He was more than happy to do that a few times a week, then go home to his Star Wars Legos. I ran the gamut with my suggestions. I asked him if he would like to play basketball, baseball, football, volleyball, and I think roller derby. He didn't care for any of it. This was a huge surprise to me because when I was a kid, I signed up for every sport whether I knew how to play or not. As kids we never even discussed it with each other. We just went to tryouts and somehow ended up on a team. I always came home from school to a group of kids playing stickball in someone's driveway. In the wintertime, each day after school, there was a touch football game on my street. Every kid had a basketball hoop in his driveway and no parent had to tell us to go play. Every free moment we had was spent playing sports. So naturally, by the time the town needed to split kids up to make teams, we just waited to get picked and continued from there.

When I was growing up, every kid had a baseball uniform, shoulder pads, and a basketball. We practiced sports every day for fun. With no adult supervision, I can honestly tell you, I was involved in some of the most violent and epic tackle football games in history. Little League was also fun because you got to face your next-door neighbor on the field. This was both great and terrifying. It was great because you both knew that whoever had a big hit would have bragging rights for the week. It was terrifying because if your next-door neighbor was the opposing pitcher, you convinced yourself that he was going to drill you in the head with the first pitch. This was mostly because all week leading up to the game your neighbor would say, "I am going to drill you in the head with the first pitch." In hindsight it is ridiculous to think that your best friend would throw a game just to send you to the hospital.

As children, we knew that if we got a pretty good group of kids together and we all played well at the same time, we could win the championship. This eternal hope and optimism got all of us through some winless seasons. It was a lot like being a Cubs fan.

There is no greater tradition between fathers and sons than going to baseball games together. For years baseball has been a common link—an unrivaled bond between the generations. My father and I started talking to each other much more frequently in my teens when he could tell me about going to World Series games in the old Polo Grounds of New York. My dad grew up idolizing Stan Musial of the Cardinals and waxed poetic about how underrated Stan the Man was as a player. (He was right, by the way. Look up the stats.)

When Jackie was four, I took him to his first big-league baseball game. It was the Dodgers versus the Astros and I had quite a surprise to lay on him once we got to the stadium. I had known Nomar Garciaparra (the two-time batting champion and '96 Rookie of the Year for the Red Sox) and his family for years and I had spoken to his parents earlier in the week so we could meet up during batting practice, say hello to Nomar, and maybe, just *maybe,* walk onto the field. Everything went perfectly. Jackie, Nik and I arrived at Dodger Stadium Chavez Ravine at 5 P.M. I called Ramon Garciaparra and told him we were ready to watch Nomar play ball. Ramon met us and handed us field-level passes. If you ever want your four-year-old to feel like a big shot, give him a ticket to hold and a pass to wear around his neck. Jackie clutched his tickets like they were the Hope Diamond and constantly checked and rechecked to be sure his pass had not blown off over his head.

While down on the field level, I allowed Jackie to drink a little soda (a big no-no in my house) while he ate his first ever Dodger dog. The Dodgers' batting practice ended and the Astros were now on the field launching monster shots over and out of the stadium. My son was more impressed with the sips of soda he was being rationed than anything baseball-related. A few moments passed when I heard "Hey, Jay!" It was Nomar, peeking up at us through the fence of the dugout. I quickly grabbed my kid and headed over.

Nomar, standing there in the whitest, cleanest uniform ever

stitched, with a giant smile, asked Jackie, "Do you still have the mitt I gave you?"

Jackie said, "Yes," and stared in awe at the superhero standing before him.

I explained to my boy that Nomar's job is to play baseball. I told him that Nomar was one of the best at his job and maybe he could teach Jackson a few things when he got older.

Jackie said, "Nomar, when I get older . . . when I grow up . . . I want to . . ." I have to interrupt here and try to explain the weight of what was about to be said. A little boy, at his first baseball game, about to tell an all-star that he wants to be a big leaguer one day is nothing short of every father's dream for his child. Jackie continued, "Nomar, when I get older . . . when I grow up . . . I want to drive machines!"

Thud.

The boy is independent, that is certain. No first-class treatment or VIP stadium parking was going to sway him from his lifelong, four-year dream of becoming a machine driver.

Nomar chuckled and said, "I think that is a great job, big man! Good for you!"

Jackie then asked the former Rookie of the Year, "Why are you wearing a belt?"

The Dodger first baseman replied, "To hold my pants up."

Jackson seemed to think that was a good answer and offered a quick "aha."

Later in the evening, Jeff Kent of the Dodgers hit a line-drive home run to left field that cleared the wall by inches. My son didn't see the pitch, he didn't see the ball hit the bat, he most certainly did not see the flight of the tiny ball clearing the fence, but he knew a party had started. The stadium went batshit, and he knew that it was his right to go batshit, too. I held him over my head as thirty thousand people screamed and cheered and the loudspeakers played rock music as Jeff Kent, my new hero, rounded the bases. I looked up at my boy as I held him to the heavens and saw a look of joy that is not possible for anyone over the age of five. His face contorted and his voice was growing hoarse from screaming. I am sure—as sure as I am sitting here typing—that if I could show people what I saw through my eyes at that moment, I could create world peace.

But when I propositioned Jackie about the possibility of being on a baseball team with a bunch of other kids he gave me a very strange answer. He said no, of course, but when I asked him why not he said, "Because what if we lose?"

What? Whose kid is this? I calmly continued with my sales pitch about the merits of winning and losing as a team. What I wanted to do was scream, *"What if you win?"*

When I was young we never thought about losing. Ever. If we were losing by ten runs and down to our last out, all we knew was that a good rally could pull it off. "What if we lose" never entered our brains. Here I was, thirty years later, being asked a very serious question. "What if we lose?" I explained to Jackie that if you lost you went back out there the next time and tried again. Then he asked, "What if you lose that time, too?" Holy shit, I am raising Eeyore. I laid off the hard sell for baseball and figured that maybe in the future my son's friends would all be piling into the local ice-cream shop with baseball uniforms on. I thought if he saw that then maybe he would think that baseball was cool. In reality he probably would have just said, "You didn't tell me we got ice cream." I thought it was a shame my boy wasn't interested in baseball. When I pitch to him in the driveway I am routinely running out into the streets to retrieve his line drives. I just can't understand for the life of me how a kid wouldn't want to make those line drives happen on an actual field before an audience.

I also tried to get Jackie to join a local basketball team but that never got past the discussion phase. As soon as I brought it up, he offered a resounding no. Before I could ask why he didn't want to play basketball he told me flat-out, "I don't like basketball." Fair enough. Football was also a no-go and I can't say that I blame him. After his being brain damaged while playing soccer, how could I convince him that football would be "fun"?

My kid likes to play alone. He likes sports where he doesn't have to share the spotlight. He likes his swimming and he loves his karate. I should also point out that despite my shouting out his athletic future in the hospital, my son is certainly not a natural athlete. After years of swim lessons, he still takes a while to realize that he knows how to swim. When he first hits the water it looks like someone dumped a pot roast into the deep end.

After I yell "Like you learned in your lessons!" he will straighten his body out and do a labored version of the freestyle. Jackie also cannot go into a pool without wearing goggles and nose plugs. I am trying desperately to wean him off these. His friends all wear them, too, though, so it's hard. Maybe I live in a pussy-kid neighborhood.

Given his early affinity for water sports, when Jackie was a little more than three years old I asked him if he wanted to come with me to rent a kayak. He said, "Um . . . no thank you." I asked him again and he declined. My feelings were hurt. I thought, Why doesn't he want to spend more time with me? and, Why can't he see how much fun we would have in a kayak together? Then I realized that maybe it's because he is three and has no fucking idea what a kayak is. I could have bent down close to his face and asked, "Wanna get a boat?" and he would have screamed "Yeah!" But no. I decided to go with the big-boy *kayak* word. While I was at it, I should have added "Let's load up on carbohydrates, fuel up on electrolytes, and navigate the Huntington Harbor tributaries." Once I explained the word *kayak* to Jackie, he was, pardon the expression, on board.

The kayak rental place is about a half mile from the beach house I was renting for the summer and the plan was to get a kayak, row to the dock behind our house, eat lunch, and then return it. Jackie and I got into the one-seater, I strapped him into his life vest, and off we went. I severely underestimated the amount of work I would be doing on the kayak, which was all of it. Jackie sat in my lap and I was having a hard time rowing without bumping him in the back of his head or clipping his shoulders. The only way to row without causing my son major head trauma was to hold the paddle against my chest and use tiny strokes. I looked like a *Tyrannosaurus rex* rowing through the harbor with my elbows behind me and my teeth showing from exertion. After forty freaking minutes, we arrived at the floating dock behind my house. I was exhausted and Jackie was very, very bored. We went into the house and I fed him some macaroni and cheese.

After lunch, I remembered that I had to bring the stupid kayak back to the rental place. There was no way I was going to row another half mile in the heat back through the harbor but because I am a genius, I decided to put the kayak in the back of my truck and drive back to the rental hut. The problem with this scenario was that my truck was at the rental place. Doh. My only other option was to put the kayak on my back and carry it like an ant. I decided to row. I left my son to Nik and his Legos and I began to row back. The currents I had fought on the way there were now much worse coming from my house. After another forty minutes (I could row using the full length of my arms now), I saw the beach where I had to return the kayak. The kayak rental man stood on the beach, waving his arms for me to bring it in. As I approached him, I was frozen with fear for a moment as I realized what I was doing. I left the kayak place with a three-year-old. I was returning with an empty life vest and a pair of children's Mickey Mouse flip-flops. This guy is going think I'm the next Scott Peterson!

I began to mentally prepare for the conversation. Should I holler from thirty yards out that I brought my son home? Should I wait for him to bring it up? Will he bring it up? Should I say "What kid?" after he asks?

I pull the kayak up to the beach and tuck the kid's life vest under my arm as the rental guy approaches and says, "Where's the little guy?"

"I dropped him off."

"Oh. That will be ten dollars for the two hours."

What the fuck!? I take a child out to sea, return without that child, and all it costs me is ten bucks? I started to wonder if the guy was going to wait until after I left to call the cops. On some strange level, I *wanted* him to think I dropped a kid off in the ocean just because I was freaked-out about how nonchalant he was.

I said, "Wow, ten bucks is pretty cheap. How about I give you fifty bucks and you let me wipe my prints off the kayak?"

The dope says, "Uh . . . no. Ten bucks is cool."

Let this rant serve as a notice to that dumb fuck Scott Peterson. If he wanted to get away with double murder, he should have gotten his lazy ass out of Modesto and rented a kayak in Huntington Beach.

So, karate it is. This seems to be what Jackie both enjoys the most and what he is best at. By the time you read this he will have become a blue belt. That's pretty badass for a seven-year-old. I'm forty and I don't even have a white belt (or a uniform). The instructors at Jackie's dojo are two of the most impressive men I have ever met. They are accomplished black belts, great teachers, and always prepared with a fun lesson plan. Most important, these men are incredibly kind.

When our children get older and life starts throwing them curveballs, it is always a relief to run into people who want the best for them. Sensei Davis and Sensei Herzog are as good as they come. I have proof of this every time my son hugs them hello and good-bye at karate class. I remember when he had his first big test for a yellow belt. The sensei lowered a screen from the ceiling of the dojo so that no one could watch the belt testing. A few nervous parents huddled closely, hoping to catch a glimpse of their child mid-belt. I was very confident that Jackie would pass. He practiced a lot at home. As I waited, I heard the instructor say, "Jackie, give me ten push-ups!" Uh-oh. What the hell was going on back there? My kid was blowing a test to become a yellow belt? After about an hour, child after child walked out from behind the screen smiling huge and wearing a new, bright yellow belt. I was relieved when Jackie came out wearing his belt. He was smiling a smile I hadn't really seen on him before. I couldn't figure out what was different about this smile from all the others I had seen in his five years. Then I realized that this smile was different because it was a smile of pride. My son was proud of himself. It is a moment I will treasure forever. I will also forever treasure the following conversation we had on the car ride home.

"Jackie, what was the hardest part of your yellow belt test?"

"Not talking."

He is definitely my son.

Jackie successfully tested for his orange and purple belts, too. After each test I would ask him that same question. Each time he would give me the same answer: "Not talking." When he was testing for his purple belt, I kept hearing the sensei tell him to do push-ups. I heard "Jackie, give me ten push-ups!" four or five times. After he came out with his new belt around his waist, I asked the sensei, "Why did Jackie have to do so many push-ups?" The sensei politely told me, "He couldn't stop talking." I asked who he was talking to. Sensei Davis told me, "No one. He was supposed to be meditating facing the wall and he was just talking to it."

Maybe it's best Jackie doesn't play football.

No matter what you want for your children, you can't control what they want for themselves. I desperately wanted my son to be a switch-hitting centerfielder and to be eluding corners out on the football field. Instead I have a very sensitive and kind boy (with the brain of a scientist) who likes to practice karate alone in front of a mirror. And I wouldn't trade him for anyone in the world.

12

KIDS CAN BE COMPETITIVE PRICKS

Why do kids have to be the absolute best at everything? I always told myself I wasn't going to be one of those pussy dads who let their kids win races or beat them at basketball in the driveway. I figured as a result, I would be building toward an incredible moment of posterity when my kid finally beat me on his own. This works in theory but when put into practice it completely backfires. After a few hundred dunks on a Nerf basketball hoop and after violently blocking every shot your kid puts in the air, eventually he doesn't want to play with you anymore. Kids are little quitters. If you don't let these pansies win every once in a while, they lose interest. I figured after Jackie had run up a record of 0-75, he would knuckle down and really start to focus on beating me. It didn't work that way.

Realistically, you can do the violent blocked shot only two or three times before your kid cries. Even those precious few blocks have to be done simultaneously with an ape impression and then an immediate fake ankle injury. Kids love when grown-ups get hurt. In fact few things are funnier to a five-year-old than when Daddy falls to the ground with a pulled hamstring. The pulled hamstring is sadly a distant second to Daddy bumping his head. If your kid is feeling blue or battling a flu, may I recommend whacking your skull on an open kitchen cabinet? Hilarity will ensue. You may need a few stitches but your child will be laughing his head off. I need to point out here that this does not work with moms. Mommy getting hurt is for some reason terrifying and never to be laughed at. Daddy getting hurt is a great afternoon.

Sometimes I'll be walking the dog with Jackie and he will say something to me like "I am so fast, Daddy. I bet I am faster than you."

I then calmly explain that it is a scientific impossibility for him to be faster than I am.

He continues: "You don't understand, Daddy. I'm so fast, I can even beat Teresa!" (That would be "Saint Teresa," our nanny.)

Oh, that's it, I get it. When he is with Teresa, she lets him win at stuff like Chutes and Ladders and footraces. The longer I think about this, the more irrational I become. I picture Jackie and his nanny running along the beach, perfectly lit like a Hallmark card. They run in slow motion with her in the lead and right as they reach the finish line she slows down and lets him waddle past. I also picture them playing tennis and her acting like she can't return his blistering serve of three miles per hour. I imagine the two of them playing basketball and her not blocking his shots. She probably just lets the kid run the lane without her ever putting a body on him or giving a good hard foul as he goes up with the ball. Basically, I envision Teresa regularly undoing all of the hard work that I am doing to raise a tough-minded, red-assed American athlete. As I think about all the fake races he has won and all the fake confidence other grown-ups have falsely put into his young, impressionable head, I become super competitive myself. I tell Jackie, "If you really think you can beat me, let's race from here to the mailbox."

He agrees and when he says "go," I haul ass to the mailbox. Sadly, I am running faster than I have in at least five years. I am all ass and elbows as I leave my four-year-old in the dust. I reach the mailbox in Olympic trial time. I look behind me with a giant "I told you so" smile on my face. I am winded like it's high school wrestling practice. Jackie was only a few feet from where we started and he is crying. I ask him why he is crying and he says, "I'm not crying." I realize that again I have acted like a complete asshole.

Jackie is mortified and with one forty-yard dash, I have

crushed his makeshift reality of being one of the fastest boys in the world. In hindsight, I should have just said "I bet you are super fast!" and left it at that. Some of you are also assholes and will think that I did the right thing. Maybe I did. What bothers me is that I am sure there was another way to get my point across without making my kid cry. That is one of the shitty parts about parenthood. There aren't any do-overs. You learn on the fly and do the best you can. Sometimes you hit your head, act like an ape, and make your child laugh until they cry. Other times you act like a maniacal competitive dick and make your kid cry.

Jackie was unbearable to be around during his competitive phase. If he saw his game piece falling behind in Candy Land, he would quit. If I struck him out playing baseball, he would say he didn't want to play anymore. He got so competitive that he would even challenge me on the validity of his greatness in bad stuff. Things that you would not want to take credit for, Jackie would still want all the credit for. If a friend and I were having a conversation about having terrible-smelling craps, he would interject, "My poop is the worst-smelling. No one has worse-smelling poop than me!"

How does one respond to that? Do you challenge him to a dump-off? Do you have him come in and smell your next runny mess and as he gags proudly announce, "I told you so"?

No, you don't. You just go on living life and worry about the big things like nutrition and warmth and safety. You let your kid's claim to having the smelliest dumps go unchallenged. Then when he has a playdate over, you embarrass the shit out of him by challenging his friend to a dump-off.

Still, I gotta hand it to Jackie, who *would* be a good contender in a dump-off. One week, when Jackie was four, he, Nik, and I all had a terrible flu. We had the runs and fever and vomited for four or five days straight. When I changed Jackie's diaper during that particular episode of hell, I felt so bad for him. I took great care in applying Desitin to his bum to make sure it didn't get irritated. I felt lucky to be caring for another human being who had no way of caring for himself. A human being who had the good fortune of being carefully handled by his doting father. I also thought to myself, I will never eat mustard again.

I still haven't eaten mustard since that day with Jackie's diarrhea, just like I haven't eaten sesame chicken since I cleaned out a litter box for the first time.

But that week, Nik had it the worst of the three of us. She was truly incapacitated by this virus and her fever was so high it was scary. I was on the phone with my mother relaying the flu update and at one point in the conversation, I said, "We were all sick but Nik really had it the worst."

Jackie pounced. "No, Daddy! I had it the worst. No one was sicker than me!"

Uh, okay, you win. You were the sickest. Good job.

Nik's nose is pure cartilage. It's a pretty good parlor trick when she can smash her nose flat against her face like a boxer being punched. One lazy afternoon she was showing Jackie and me how cool it was. But he was not going to be out-lack-of-boned. He stood up from the couch and announced, "I have more cartilage than you, Pretty Girl! Look. Look. Look." Each time he said "look" he pushed his nose harder against his face, trying in vain to take the most-cartilage crown.

It takes Nik a hell of a lot to argue with anyone and she certainly wasn't going to start now. She quietly told him great job on his abundance of cartilage and stood up to go do something, anything, else.

I thought I could bring my aggressively competitive son back to earth by talking to him about sharks. I told him, "You know, Jackie, sharks are made up of only cartilage. They have no bones in their bodies at all. They are *all* cartilage. Isn't that cool?"

Jackie said, "They don't have more cartilage than me, Daddy." He was now pressing his nose against his face like a special person with OCD. "Look, Daddy, look how much cartilage I have. No one has more cartilage than me!"

I said, "Jackie, a shark is made of cartilage. They don't have any bones."

He interrupted, "No one has more cartilage than me, Daddy! I have the most cartilage, look!" Pressing his nose in hard against his face, he looked like an old saloonkeeper.

Later that night I put him down to bed and walked out of

the room. As I lay next to Nik in bed, we heard through the monitor, "Daddy?"

I walked down the hallway into his room, leaned over his crib, and asked, "Yeah?"

Jackie said, "My nose hurts."

Our kids are mysteries. We try but we never really know what they are thinking. We tell our children that they are going to have a sleepover at their best friend's house. Five minutes later we see our daughter with a big smile on her face. We'll be proud of ourselves for arranging the sleepover. We'll ask our child, "What are you smiling about?"

The kid will answer, "Penguins."

Of course you are.

We push: "Aren't you excited about the sleepover I put together?"

She responds, "What sleepover?"

The insanity continues.

We don't know what our kids are thinking and we really never know what they think of us. We don't really know what our parents think of us, either. As I have gotten older I have realized that this is a good thing. Throughout my youth, my parents superbly hid the fact that I was a major pain in the ass and that they were afraid I was going to amount to nothing. That's a lot to filter through when you're ten, so Mom and Dad, thank you for keeping it from me until I was eleven.

Jackson tends to play his emotions about me close to the

vest. I guess he thinks I am funny. I think he knows I love him like crazy. I am somewhat certain he knows I am very fair. But in actuality I have no idea what his concept of me is. When I finally got a glimpse into his psyche, I was stunned by what I saw.

One day after lunch, Jackie, who was six at the time, and I were walking our dog, when a black SUV pulled up next to us and I heard, "Is that Jay?"

As a rule I do not like to talk to fans or strangers when I am with my kid. I sort of ignored the voice and kept walking. Then from inside, the voice said much louder this time, "That IS Jay!" The voice sounded very familiar. I squinted against the sun and saw Chris Rock in a Range Rover. I didn't know Chris lived anywhere near my neighborhood, so I was surprised to see him. I asked him where he lived and he told me he was renting a house a few blocks southwest of me. We chatted for a while and shook hands good-bye.

Then Chris drove up the street. As his truck pulled onto Sunset Boulevard I turned to Jackie. "Did you see that man I was just talking to?"

He said, "He was nice."

I agreed. I then asked, "You know how I have a comedy job? I tell jokes and funny stories to people at night?"

"Uh-huh."

I bent down. "That man that just drove away is the funniest man in the world. He is the best. No one is funnier than him. Isn't that cool? You just met the funniest man in the world."

My boy looked up at me and maybe he just had sun in his eyes but I think he was tearing up.

I asked him what was wrong and he said, "I thought *you* were the funniest man in the world."

You could have knocked me over with a feather. Jackie rarely laughs at a single thing I say. When I do impressions or funny voices he will often tell me, "It's quiet time, Daddy."

Now, suddenly, in the middle of the street with the sun in our eyes, I find out that my kid thinks I am the funniest man in the world. I explained to Jackie that I am very good at my job but no one is as good as Chris Rock. He is the absolute best there is.

Looking puzzled, he said, "But he didn't say anything funny."

I explained that when Chris Rock goes to his comedy job at night he says funny things the whole time.

Jackie said, "How long does he say them?"

I said, "About an hour."

"How long do you say them?"

"The same, about an hour."

"Maybe if you said them for two hours instead of one hour then you would be the funniest."

I stated emphatically that no matter how long I told jokes for, or no matter where I told them, I would never be as funny as Chris Rock. "He's just the best."

You could practically hear the gears grinding in my Jackie's head. First of all, his father was admitting to being completely outclassed by someone with the same job. Second, his father didn't seem to mind that he was outclassed by someone with the same job. It was a big moment for the kid. Perhaps this competitive thing was overrated after all.

A little later in the walk I could see that Jackie was still processing all this information.

I whispered to him, "Remember that funniest guy in the world we just met?"

"Yeah."

"I can totally beat him in a race."

Several minutes later, Jackie said, "But you can't beat me in a race, Daddy!"

This time I was ready to let my child bring home the gold. I said, "Okay, Jackie boy, on three . . ."

When will children stop falling for the "on three" trick? All parents know this trick. It usually involves a Band-Aid. You tell your daughter that you will take the Band-Aid off "on three" and then you rip it off on two. As your child gets older and a little wiser, you rip it off on one. When she is seven you have to start saying, "Okay, I'm gonna take it off on the count of RIIIP!!!"

The last time I tried the "on three" trick was when Jackie was six and had a loose tooth. He asked me if I could tie a string around his tooth and tie the other end of the string to the closet door to rip it out. This is something that grown-ups usually threatened me with when I was a kid. I always declined. Now my son was actually requesting it. I thought I was hallucinating.

I found some string in the laundry room and tied it around my boy's tooth. If you want to laugh, try tying string around a tooth. I don't know why, but it was hilarious. The string kept coming off when I tried to double-knot it and Jackie has never held his mouth that open for that long in his life. There was an enormous and constant ribbon of drool from his bottom lip to the floor. I finally got both sides of the string secured and told him, "Okay, Jackie, on three." I slammed the door shut on two. The string broke. The string broke the next time I tried it, too. The third time I tried it, I still told Jackie, "On three," and the poor guy believed me. This time I anticipated him bracing himself on the number two so I slammed the closet door on one. This time the tooth flew out of his mouth and made a "ping" as it hit the closet doorknob. We were successful. Except for the part that the tooth was nowhere near ready to come out. I should have waited at least a week to pull it. But when a child asks you to yank a tooth out of his mouth, you must take advantage of the situation.

The blood began to flow instantly. It kept flowing and flowing because the tooth should have still been in my son's head and not on the end of a string hanging from a door. Like most humans, kids associate blood with bad news. Jackie is no different. I grabbed some toilet paper and told him to press down real hard where his tooth used to be. I explained that this would help the grown-up tooth know where to come in.

My God, this kid's jaw was spewing blood like he got shot at Normandy!

Eventually the bleeding subsided a little and Jackie fell asleep. I convinced him that it would be a good idea to sleep with the toilet paper still pressed to his gums so the tooth fairy would know he was the guy to give money to.

At about one in the morning Jackie tapped me awake. "Daddy, I'm bleeding again." I opened my eyes and there was a freaking blood-covered zombie standing in front of me. The entire bottom part of his face was stained red with blood. I thought, My God, *True Blood!* Go hang upside down or something! I again convinced my child that all of this blood was completely normal and told him that the more a tooth bleeds, the more money the tooth fairy will give you. By the morning, the tooth fairy had left him five bucks.

The next time my son showed me a loose tooth I asked him if he wanted to get some string.

Before I could finish the sentence, he sternly said, *"No."*

13

PUNISHMENT

It seems that as the years go by, children get punished less than they used to. This goes back hundreds of years. Back in the 1800s, if you were bad, you had to go chop wood by yourself in the woods with the Indians. These days we give our kids time-outs, take away their Nintendo DS, and try other bullshit "punishments." Is it because kids today are better behaved than kids from years past? Hell no! Kids today are completely spoiled and have way too much say in everything.

"Kids should be seen but not heard" is a popular saying from the good old days. Most parents wish this were still preached. In my house, I have to wait for a pause in one of Jackson's rambling Pokémon stories to get a sentence in. The second my sentence is finished he starts up where he left off again. I am a visitor in my own house. How did this happen?

I think it started long before I was even a parent. As the years go by, each generation of parents punishes their kids a little less harshly than the generation prior. Subsequently, every ten years or so, we have a group of new babies who are whiny pains in the ass. Do you think parents gave their kids time-outs sixty years ago? No, no, they did not. They took their belts off and beat their kids like rented mules. When I was a kid, I would have delighted in a "time-out" or having to "go straight to my room." I would have shrugged off these detriments to crime and merely spent the time alone plotting my next act of terror on the neighborhood.

I don't even believe in spanking, let alone whipping, but somewhere along the line parents and kids have to reach some sort of compromise. Parents need to be a little more forceful with their punishments and kids need to stop walking in on us having sex. I haven't worked out all the details on this but I think it's a start. Instead of the evolution of punishment, parents are witnessing the *de*-evolution of punishment.

My dad once told me that when he and my uncle Art were around twelve and eleven years old, respectively, they got into a heated argument in the backseat of my grandfather's car. My grandfather didn't threaten to turn the car around. He dropped the two of them off and drove away. They spent the next two hours running as fast as they could on the shoulder of the New

Jersey Turnpike. They stopped fighting in the car after that day. Back in the '50s, people knew to handle their kids. Drop them off on the freeway. Can you imagine if you saw two preteens running along the shoulder of the freeway where you live? You would pick them up, drive them to the police station, and have their parents arrested.

My father's father was very creative when it came to punishing his four boys. My father had a curfew that he routinely broke. At the age of ten or so, in the summertime, my dad was always to be home by seven. But every evening, he'd saunter in at around 8:30. My grandfather never said a word about it. He just kept letting my father think that he was getting away with breaking curfew every night. This went on for weeks until one night, before my dad came home, my grandfather took a FOR SALE sign off the neighbor's lawn and hammered it into his own front yard. He hid the family car down the block. He took the other three boys and my grandma upstairs and turned all the lights off. When my dad came home later that night, he rang the doorbell and knocked on the door. He peeked into the garage. He noticed the For Sale sign on the lawn. He thought the family had moved. He sat down on the front steps of the house and cried. My grandparents let him suffer out there thinking his life was over for half an hour. Finally, my grandfather opened the door and told my father to get upstairs to bed. My father never missed curfew after that.

It's important to be decisive when punishing your kids.

Never pass the buck. One day, my father and his brothers were being complete assholes to my grandma. All day she kept telling them, "Wait until your father gets home!" She said this from about noon to seven, when my grandfather came home from New York City. What my grandma did not know is that my grandfather had had one of the worst days of his life at the office. His trains were also delayed and all he wanted to do was come home and relax with his family. The moment my grandfather walked through the door my grandma let him have it. She screamed at him to go downstairs and take care of his rotten sons. She really went bananas and wasn't about to let him have a moment's rest until he doled out the punishments. My weary, exhausted grandfather walked down the steps into the basement where my grandma had banished the boys an hour earlier. As he came down the steps, they cowered in fear. He took off his belt and told them, "I am going to beat the walls with this belt. I want you guys to scream like I am a madman that has lost his mind. Can you do that?" The plan was met with excited nods of approval. My grandfather then let out a maniacal scream and began trashing the basement. He beat the walls with his fists and let picture frames smash to the ground. My dad and my uncles Kent, Bobby, and Art were screaming like they were in a horror flick. My grandma came flying down the basement steps crying, "Jack, stop it, you're going to kill them! Stop!" When she turned the corner she saw four very happy young boys sitting down and laughing. My grandfather handed her his belt and said, "Don't ever wait for me to come home to punish them again!"

The devolution of punishments doesn't even have to reach through the generations. My sisters, Virginia and Julie, are only six and five years older than me, respectively, and even they got punished more severely than I did. Maybe it's simply the fact that by the time parents have their third child they give up on discipline. Regardless of the reason, I am grateful. I was even grateful at the time. At a very young age I was aware of the fact that I was not getting spanked with the same passion as my sisters had been. Virginia and Julie tell horror stories about The Wooden Spoon. Throughout their childhoods, my mother and father were quick to reach into the kitchen drawer and pull out the cruelest weapon 23 Valley View Road ever saw. Each sister would have marks on the backs of her legs from just one good swat of The Wooden Spoon. By the time I was at ass-kicking age, The Wooden Spoon had more or less been retired into a docile life of mixing cake batter. It remained a threat, though. When I would behave particularly crazily, my mom would ask if I wanted her to get The Wooden Spoon. I did not. This question settled me down immediately.

There was, however, one lazy summer day when The Wooden Spoon had my name on it. I was about nine, and I was hanging out with a neighborhood kid named Jeff, who was about twelve. Jeff lived in the house behind mine and since he was older, I always felt lucky to be getting his attention. On this fateful day, Jeff proposed that we play a cool game (of his own invention). He said, "Okay, the object of the game is to see who can throw a mud ball closest to a moving car without hitting it. I'll go first." He missed the car by a good fifteen feet. I now knew that I could beat Jeff at his own game with just one throw. As the next car came down the street, I rifled my mud ball through the air. The driver's side window on the car was down. Technically, I won the game because I did come closest to the moving car without hitting it. I hit the driver in the face instead. The driver, after getting blasted in the face by my mud ball, locked up his brakes and skidded to a stop. He jumped out of the car, mud on his face, and looked straight at me. I turned to look at Jeff. He was gone. Older boys have an amazing ability to evaporate when shit hits the fan. The driver said, "Is this your house?" I said, "No." Then the driver (who looked like something out of a freaking monster movie) asked where I lived. I still lie awake at night and think about what happened next. I turned around, pointed behind me and said, "I live in that blue house right there. Number twenty-three." The man got back in his car, did a donut and headed over to the blue house, number 23.

The mud ball gag was probably my worst childhood offense. I knew that as soon as this guy got to my house with that scary mud face I would be beaten senseless. I knew The Wooden Spoon would be taken out of retirement for my ass. My plan was simple, if flawed. I would just not go home until my parents went to sleep and forgot about me. During my few hours on the

Iam, I told every kid in the neighborhood what I had done and how much trouble I was going to be in. I was a local celebrity for the day. Kids from a few streets away showed up because they heard I had mud-balled a car and was going to be beaten to death by my parents. At about seven in the evening, I broke down and started to walk home. I looked like the Pied Piper of Valley View Road with about fifteen kids trailing behind me. I walked solemnly and slowly as the mob behind me laughed and cheered. As I came down my street, I saw the mud ball car parked crookedly in my driveway. I was dead. When I came into the house to face the music, everyone was in the living room waiting for me. The second that mud ball guy saw me, he made the ID. "Yep, that's him." And then he walked out of the house. I was doomed. My mother leapt from her chair and told me to get to my room. As I walked upstairs, I could hear my mother opening kitchen drawers behind me. I was going to be killed.

Through my bedroom window I could see that the neighborhood kids had gathered in the backyard. They were pointing up to my window, shoving each other and laughing. I could also hear them chanting my name. My reverie was broken when my mother crashed through the door with the weapon concealed behind her back. I began to think about what I wanted people to say at my funeral. As my mother reached out to beat me, I noticed the spoon was absent. By some miracle from God, she couldn't find it! Instead, she began to spank my ass with one of those cheap balsa wood rulers that come with cans of paint. I had gotten lucky.

As my mom started to rain blows upon my backside, I was immediately amazed by the fact that this cheap ruler did not hurt at all. A bare hand would have hurt more. But I knew that the more my mother *thought* she was hurting me, the faster the whole ordeal would be over with. So I screamed as loud as I could. I screamed like my father and my uncles had screamed decades earlier. I begged for my life. I begged for mercy. When my mom finished, she said, "Now get outside!"

As I stepped out, all the neighborhood kids stared at me in stunned silence. They had never heard such a violent beating before. I wanted to let the older kids know that I was tough though, so I said, "It didn't hurt!" This apparently was the funniest thing ever said. They had all heard me scream. They heard me beg for my life. No one believed me when I explained that I was just pretending. It only made them laugh harder. Years later I realized that what had happened in my bedroom that summer was my first successful acting scene.

I am fairly certain that my son will never meet a wooden spoon unless he is baking a cake. Fortunately, Jackson is a very good boy, which is a godsend, because I am an absolutely terrible disciplinarian. My punishments are always poorly timed and my intentions misunderstood. The only person who ever seems to learn a lesson is me.

A few years ago, Jackson and I were visiting Nik at work

on the set of her television show *Las Vegas*. She gave Jackie a Big Bird PEZ dispenser, which he flipped over. He was rarely allowed to eat candy and now not only was he given a free pass to eat candy but it was shooting out of Big Bird's mouth. He was in heaven. But about halfway through the day, Jackie started to get ornery. He was complaining and whining and generally disagreeable. Since this kind of behavior is so out of character, I let it slide for a while.

Eventually I said simply, "Knock it off."

He replied simply, "No!"

I was stunned. "Jackie, do not ever speak to me that way. If you do, I am going to throw away your Big Bird PEZ dispenser."

Again, he said, "No!"

I continued to warn him that the more he acted like a brat, the closer he was to getting his Big Bird PEZ dispenser thrown in the garbage.

On the drive home, he started kicking the back of my seat.

I said, "Jackie, stop kicking my seat."

"*No!*"

I pulled the car to the side of the road and pulled the Big Bird PEZ dispenser out of his hands. When I spotted a garbage can, I rolled down my window, tossed the thing out, and drove away. It actually felt pretty good—like I had finally arrived at parenthood. I disciplined my son without hitting or causing confusion. I warned him all day that if he kept it up I was going to throw away the Big Bird PEZ dispenser.

As we drove on, Nik asked calmly, "I know you were upset with Jackie, but what did I do wrong?"

"Nothing. You didn't do anything wrong. Why?"

"You just threw out my Big Bird PEZ dispenser."

I explained that I had used it as a bartering tool earlier in the day and I couldn't go back on my word.

Nik went on, calmer still. "No, what I mean is, that was *my* Big Bird PEZ dispenser. I have had it since I was Jackie's age. My dad gave it to me when I was three years old."

Gulp. (And those Coxes! They save every stinkin' toy!)

By now we were well onto the freeway and there was no going back to retrieve Big Bird. I wanted to teach my son a lesson and my wife wound up as collateral damage. To this day I haven't been able to find another Big Bird PEZ dispenser. It wouldn't have the sentimental value but it'd be better than nothing. If you are reading this and happen to have one, please mail it to me care of Simon & Schuster. You can also send cash. Actually, just send cash.

Parents, child psychologists, and Dr. Phil all weigh in very passionately on whether or not to spank. It is a hotly debated issue. It wasn't always. Anyone reading this book who is at least thirty years old no doubt had parents who had no problem giving out a spanking at the drop of a hat. I once spoke to a child psychologist who asked me if I believed in hitting children. I told her no, I do not believe in hitting children . . . but I do believe in spanking. The therapist tried to convince me that "hitting" and "spanking" were the same thing. I see her point, but I disagree. Not to be obvious about it or anything, but hitting is hitting and spanking is spanking; and to me, they are apples and oranges. I believe in spanking a child—*once.*

My theory on spanking is much like the theory of nuclear proliferation. You drop the bomb once and every once in a while after that you show a few satellite photos of your silos. Our country has an enormous arsenal of nuclear weapons and I have very large hands. Every once in a while, some rogue country will get a chip on its shoulder and start acting like an asshole to the United States. That's when we remind that country of the damage we once did, a long time ago, and they subsequently back off. I spanked my son *once* on his diapered bottom when he was two and a half. It was for hitting his babysitter in the face. (Notice I didn't say "spanking his babysitter in the face." See?)

The first time, I hollered, "No, Jackie! We do *not* hit people!" After my first reprimand, a few moments went by and again Jackie hit the babysitter. So I spanked his bottom once with my hand. To say he was shocked would be quite the understatement. My son looked lost and it absolutely broke my heart to see but it laid the framework for a worst-case scenario that he now has to refer to for the rest of his life.

Virginia Woolf once wrote, "Children never forget injustice. They forgive heaps of things grown-up people mind; but that sin is the unpardonable sin." I agree with that. When I spanked Jackie that one time, he no doubt found it to be a grand injustice. Hopefully, he will never forget it. When he has days where he is going bananas and nothing I say calms him down or gets him to behave, all I have to do is ask him, "Do you need to be spanked?" This question stops my son dead in his tracks every time. Psychologists might argue that I have taught my son that "hitting" is okay because I spanked him as a result of his behavior. Maybe they are right, but my son behaves like an angel when the subject of my hand comes up.

I was spanked fairly regularly as a kid. My parents were not at all abusive. The fact of the matter is that I was *bad*. I did not listen to anything that anyone told me, and many times the only way to truly get me to pay attention was to smack my ass with a hand. Also, my parents had two rules in their home that, if broken, were met with a swift and severe ass-kicking. Rule number one was *Do not lie to us*. Rule number two was *Do not ever, ever, ever, lie to us!* I got spanked with my pants down in front of the neighbors if I lied. If parents tried that today the local news would be on our streets with a lead story about the pedophile who is torturing children. I don't know what the solution is but we definitely should be able to punish our kids without fear of being taken to court.

The lying spankings always commenced immediately, before the punctuation was put on the lie. In retrospect, my sisters and I were fine with this arrangement and it was with grave and meticulous thought that the rule was ever broken. My problem was that I did so many bad things to so many different people that I had to keep a bank vault full of lies to cover my tracks at any given interrogation.

The issue of spanking is a big reason I am glad I don't have girls. I couldn't bring myself to spank a little girl for the one-time allotment. It is, however, safe to say that if I did have a baby girl, I would quickly be bankrupt. How can you say no to those eyes and those little voices? I would be doomed. I can picture myself sitting there with my daughter when she pipes up, "Daddy, I want a zebra!" My first thought would be, Okay, how much does a zebra cost? We could keep it in the yard. We'll paint it brown and tell the neighbors it's a Great Dane.

I only have a boy, so I obviously have no idea what it would be like to raise a girl. I imagine that boys are easier. When boys raise their voices and yell "No!" at you, you can give them a mean, ice-cold stare in an attempt to get them to respect your strength and authority. If my little girl raised her voice and yelled "No!" I would think, Oh my God, she is *so* cute!

Nik told me once that she was never spanked as a kid. When I accused her of not telling me the truth, she said, "I was never spanked until I asked to be." Nice (and sexy) comeback. I think that boys are probably easier to raise than girls, in general. Let's say, hypothetically, that you have three boys. One day they are all on sugar highs and generally acting like aggressive idiots. You can yell, "Enough! Go outside and play in the yard!" Your boys will most likely shrug their shoulders and mosey outside and continue their battle royal. Conversely, if you have three girls and they are acting crazy and shrieking and arguing and you yell, "Enough! Go outside and play in the yard!" the girls would look at you like you are the king of the interlopers and say something like "Why don't *you* go outside? You are so stupid, Dad! Why don't you cut the grass like Mommy asked you to so we could find the lawn to play on? Duh!" followed by a smattering of "He's so gay!" and "No wonder Mommy eats!"

I like the boy scenario better. Boys may get mad at you but they will forgive and forget the moment you put a plate of pasta and turkey meatballs in front of them. Girls, like most women, are not quick to forgive and definitely won't forget. And as you sleep, they will plan your funeral.

I don't spank my kid, because I think as a form of punishment, spanking is archaic and just plain old terrible. Don't get me wrong, I see some kids in the mall who definitely need their asses whupped; I just don't believe in spanking *my* kid. I speak from experience when I say that spanking instills a lifetime of confusion, fear, and embarrassment. I get sick when I hear parents talk about how once they spanked their kids, they started behaving. Maybe that's true but those parents also rendered their kids scared shitless whenever they walk into the room. I would rather command respect from my child than fear. By the way, does anyone else think that the word *spank* is beginning to sound funny?

My timing is bad when it comes to punishment. Around the same year as the Big Bird Incident, there was one day that Jackie was acting like a total creep. If I asked him to sit down, he stood up. If I told him to follow me, he would lie down on the ground. I couldn't figure out why he was being so insolent. I told him he needed a nap and he was going to take it immediately. He fought me on it. He cried and carried on and turned into Baby with No Bones. I lifted him up by his hands and set him down on his bed. What I did next I really regret, but I yelled my fucking head off. I looked at my three-year-old and really let him have it. I told him he was acting like a total creep and I wouldn't stand for it. I put him in a time-out in his room for a full hour (which is about four days, in toddler time). When I came back into Jackie's room, he was asleep. When he awoke, he was burning up with a 103° fever. I was crushed that I had acted like such an asshole. Jackson was obviously grouchy because he was sick as a dog.

The problem with three-year-olds is that they rarely say "I don't feel well. I think I'm getting sick." Instead they get incredibly grouchy and insolent. If I had a DeLorean and could go back in time, I would take Jackson's temperature instead of losing my temper.

When our children are sick we feel so helpless. By the time they're four or five, it isn't so bad, because they communicate better about what the problem is. But when they are babies, it is just a long, never-ending cry. You get angry and frustrated that they are crying so hard, and when the doctor tells you they have the flu you feel like a real shit for being annoyed in the first place. And it's hard to learn and remember after only one time even though that seems like the logical thing to do.

I remember another time that Jackie had been crying for two straight days and I was ready to leave him at a Dodgers game. Finally I took him to the pediatrician.

Oh, the pediatrician! Obviously you have to take your child regularly to a good pediatrician (not just when they are sick, like this time). It isn't like having a puppy, where you delay the appointments for months on end. Babies need constant care. I'm not even talking about the constant yammering about food and water that they do. They need vaccinations and regular checkups to make sure they are growing the right way. Measuring and weighing the baby is a constant. It's as if once you have a baby, every person becomes a sideshow carnival worker. You approach a bench at the playground and the guy next to you says, "What is that baby, about sixteen months? He weighs around twenty pounds? What is that thing, twenty-eight inches?"

If the guy is close, am I supposed to give him a stuffed puma or a SpongeBob shot glass? Fuck off, mister, get away from my baby. You're creepy. Grown-ups don't play this Guess-Your-Weight game. We have learned that this is incredibly rude and annoying. Imagine meeting a new guy at work who shakes your hand and says, "What are you, about forty? One hundred forty-five pounds? Five foot three? You're pretty big. Are you in the upper percentile?" You'd knock that guy out. You wouldn't lean over and guess back. But that is what grown-ups do with babies.

It's fun to freak people out and give them incorrect information. When a mom at the park leans over your kid's stroller and says, "How old is he, eight months?" You should reply, "Nope. Fourteen. Fourteen years old. I am completely freaked out. I think maybe a valve didn't open up or something. Do you have any advice?" It's fun to go the other way, too. The next time you are playing catch with your three-year-old and some fat, nosybody comes up and asks, "Is he three? Four?" Just deadpan to the person, "Ten months. I don't know what I'm feeding him. He freaks me out. I would ditch him, but he drove here."

Unless your baby is actually ill, it seems that a pediatrician's main job is just to measure and weigh the baby. You make the appointment a few months in advance. When it comes time for the appointment, you pack the baby's stuff into the car, you get the baby into the car seat. You drive all the way across town. You find parking. You lug all your baby stuff (and the baby) into the office. You sign in. You wait . . . and wait. Finally the receptionist tells you that you can go wait in another room. You wait in the other room for another ten minutes until the doctor is ready for you. She then puts your baby on a scale, takes out a tape measure, and hands the baby back. She'll exclaim, "Thirty inches. Twenty-eight pounds!" then walk out. Thanks for coming. Try the veal. Tip your waitress. See the receptionist on your way out to make another electrifying appointment for six months from now.

I have always had a bit of a phobia about the pediatrician's office. All those toys they stack up in the waiting room skeeve me out. There are always very old board games, too. A twenty-year-old game of Parcheesi with writing on the board sits in the toy chest. All the pieces have been chewed down to different-colored nubs by sick babies. A good pediatrician's waiting room should have a ton of Elmo toys, a Thomas the Tank Engine set—with the Thomas table (don't make my kid drag magnetic trains through the carpet because you're cheap). A Scooby Doo mystery machine is awesome to have but not a deal breaker. No more board games. Two-year-olds don't want to play Yahtzee before their flu shot. Most important, make sure you have gallons of Purel. I better see a wall-mounted Purel the second I walk in. If I don't, I am taking my business elsewhere. Imagine how many sick babies have had all of those toys in their sick mouths! It is truly disgusting. There are teeth marks and dried snot on every toy in the waiting room. The freaking crayons have been eaten. Doctors, replace your crayons every five years, will you? I don't want my baby girl holding half a chewed-up crayon as some other kid craps the other half into his diaper across town.

I know the toys are for the sick babies to play with and I am grateful for them. I just think there should be an alternate group of toys as well. Maybe a shelf filled with Vicks VapoRub and a big fountain of liquid Benadryl. All the kids in the waiting room could have a blast sliming each other up with VapoRub, drinking from the Benadryl fountain and laughing as they draw faces on the first baby to fall asleep.

Also, when are we allowed to stop referring to our children's ages in months? It's getting a little ridiculous. You are at a birthday party and while inside the jumpy you ask a dad, "How old is your daughter?" The guy says, "She's thirty six months." What a dick.

I always say back, "Wow, she looks three." As of this writing I am 450 months old. I still don't want to play Yahtzee before a flu shot.

I had a strange experience when I had to bring my son in to the pediatrician for his two-year checkup. This is a big checkup. Your baby gets a few shots, gets weighed, gets measured. But afterward, the doctor doesn't clap her hands and walk out like a blackjack dealer. Instead, at the two-year checkup, she studies the baby, then compares him to every other baby that has ever spit up. After she has bell-curved the shit out of your baby, she tells you what percentile he is in. In the pediatrician's office you want your kid to routinely bang out ninetieth percentiles. If they grade lower it is always a long and depressing car ride home. You ask them over and over, "Why can't you just grow more?" They face the back of the car and drool.

The problem with pediatricians is that instead of telling you everything you should do for your kid in the time leading up to the next visit, they tell you all the shit you did wrong since the last visit. When my son was on the scale during his two-year checkup, I actually heard the pediatrician gasp. She didn't even try to hide it. She just let out this weird yelp and then turned to me and said, "Your baby weighs thirty pounds! That is too heavy!" I had thought that a pudgy-wudgy baby was a sign of health. I was wrong. Apparently, my son was alarmingly heavy for a two-year-old. I never really thought about this before but it did explain my backaches and suddenly bulging arm muscles.

The pediatrician was alarmed by my baby's weight and she began to make me feel like a lousy parent. She asked, "You're not still feeding him baby food, are you?" Uh, yeah, I was. She began to shout, "No! No! No! He's twenty-four-months old!" (What a bitch. It's called the *two-year* checkup.) She went on. "By twenty months he should be eating solids! He should have pasta and carrots and grapes and bananas and bread!"

I thought, Well, you never told me that, you dumb quack! I was just here six months ago; you might have mentioned something about my son's need to chew on your way out of the room. But you didn't. So as a result of your negligence, I am giving my poor guy six jars of baby food per sitting. Each meal I mix the jars together and it is a little too thick, so I add whole milk. Then it's too thin, so I add oatmeal. Then it's too thick, so I add milk again. Eventually, I add in some Myoplex and keep stirring until it is all just right. I'm like the new version of Goldilocks—Daddylocks. Every day and night I deliver this vat o' baby food to the big, fat mafia boss in the high chair. I struggle to get the bowl up onto his tray and my son just sits there rubbing his belly with his sausage fingers. I had no idea this was bad for the poor kid. No wonder he looks like the bottom part of a snowman!

The pediatrician didn't have to go through all that percentile crap just to shout at me in front of my kid. She saw damn well when we came in here it looked like I was holding the number eight. Next the doctor asked, "Is he crawling yet?" That's when I lost it. "No, he can't crawl! Look at him. He can barely blink! He just rolls around the house. When I need him for something I just go and pick him up!" Apparently, I'm in the first percentile of parents.

The day that I took Jackie for his two-year checkup he cried for two days straight, though the doctor made herself useful by diagnosing him with "a terrible cold." She prescribed some cough medicine and told me how and when to administer it.

It was grape-flavored and I tasted it first. (You never know, it might have codeine in it and if so, Daddy might also have a terrible cold.) After tasting Jackie's grape cough medicine, I gave him the recommended dose, put him to sleep, and walked upstairs to my kitchen, where I had a bunch of grapes sitting in a bowl on the counter. I quickly popped a grape into my mouth to see how much it tasted like Jackie's medicine.

It tasted nothing at all like the medicine. I realized right then and there that the people who make anything "grape-flavored" have really pulled the wool over our eyes. Their products taste like purple! The geniuses at all the pharmaceutical companies have effectively figured out what colors taste like.

Cherry-flavored medicine tastes red. It doesn't taste anything at all like actual cherries. Eat a cherry and then have a cherry-flavored antacid. They taste nothing alike.

Anyway . . . it is hard to train yourself to realize that babies' cries are the only way they have to communicate. Rarely will a baby cry for crying's sake. They are either hungry or wet or have a fever. Sometimes your son is whining like a little bitch because he has a 104° fever. And sometimes your son is being an insolent little brat because he's two and a half and he's good at his job. As I said earlier, Nik and I don't really have any real discipline problems in our house. Our son likes to play quietly by himself and it's hard to punish a loner and give him a time-out. Jackie has a whole playroom for himself and some days he spends more than two hours working on a Lego creation. If Nik or I call him for dinner, he walks to the bathroom, washes his hands, and sits down to eat. We're lucky. Some parents are not as lucky. We all know someone whose kids are assholes. *Those* kids need to be spanked. If you have to, and I mean *really* have to spank your kid, I suggest doing it early while they are still wearing diapers. The diaper is a good natural pad for the butt that can also act as a buffer for light spanks.

Our parents love to tell us horror stories about how bad their punishments were when they were kids. What will our children tell their kids? "When I was your age and was bad, I had to sit in a chair in my room for five whole minutes." Some kids today don't even have a time limit on their time-outs. The parents say, "You go in there and don't come out until you are sorry!" My grandmother tried this on me once when I was staying overnight at her house. I walked out of the room two minutes later and said, "I'm sorry" and she made me a sandwich. There is just too much talking between parents and kids. Your five-year-old should not have the floor for a few minutes to explain his point of view. That is how you raise creeps and lawyers.

14

SNIP, SNIP, HOORAY!

Kids in this world are cruel. Regardless of how well we safe-guard our children against bullies, they will still be bullied. Take it from me, a guy who had the shit kicked out of him plenty: Bullies are incredible at their job. If a bully decides he feels like kicking your ass, you are getting your ass kicked. Some days it happens for no reason at all except that it's just your turn in the barrel. Bullies are as good with verbal beatings as they are with physical beatings. Whoever came up with the expression "adding insult to injury" was probably watching a bully at work. If a creep at school doesn't feel like mustering up the energy to knock your teeth out, he will spend weeks ripping your self-esteem out. Bullies are like heat-seeking missiles when it comes to imperfections. Any perceived weakness your child has will be identified by the school asshole and ridiculed regularly. If a kid two classrooms away has a bunch of freckles, a bully can sense it. A bully can feel a fat kid approaching on a school bus. Whatever it is these animals decide is our flaw, they go after it until we break.

In my high school there were two uncircumcised boys. I am almost forty years old and I still remember their names. Chris Lowell and Brian Connolly, or, more affectionately, Anteater and Eggroll. These poor guys were teased mercilessly. Every day while changing for gym class or wrestling practice, the hilarity ensued. Every. Single. Time. It just never got old. Someone would always holler out, "Hey! Get a look at Eggroll!" or "The Anteater has arrived!"

Brian Connolly was on the wrestling team, so we all saw him and his eggroll every day when we dutifully lined up naked for weigh-ins. As the other team would line up on the other side of the locker room, we would tease, "It's your turn to get on the scale, Eggroll!" Then we would all laugh and high-five. (In hindsight, it was all pretty gay. Boys staring at other boys' dicks and high-fiving.)

I can remember one evening in the locker room after a loss, everyone was dejected and brooding. Every wrestler on the team had lost with the exception of our heavyweight, Mickey Burns. Mickey was an absolute savage and probably should have been caged in a zoo. He wrestled at 200 pounds, which meant that that was the weight he got *down* to. He probably walked around at about 230 in the summer. Mickey Burns was the only kid in town who had ever been arrested for fighting. Twice. The second arrest came when he went across the desk at a guidance counselor for calling him a juvenile. Mickey Burns thought the guy was calling him a Jew so he attacked him (true story). Bottom line is that Mickey Burns was *not* to be fucked with.

Brian Connolly wrestled at 140 pounds. After this particular match, Brian Connolly was sitting on a bench with a towel around his waist and his face in his hands. Mickey, who moments earlier had driven his opponent into the center of the earth, patted Brian on the back and said, "Cheer up, Eggroll." Brian Connolly stood up, and then butt-ass naked, drilled Mickey in the face with a lightning-fast right cross and knocked him out cold. Mickey had never lost a fight in his life and now here he lay unconscious on the cold tile floor of the locker room with an uncircumcised cock flapping above him. As the ambulance came and carried him—naked and unconscious— out into the snowy night, we all decided to go with the name Brian from that day forward.

Why put your kid through torture in his teens when he has enough to worry about? Why not just put him through torture when he is a baby and has nothing to worry about? Now I realize that circumcision may not be the moral of the bully story in general, but please circumcise your child. I know that it is purely cosmetic and there is no medical reason for it. I know your baby will cry and scream while it is being done. But in the long run, it will all work itself out. Having my son circumcised was an easy decision and one I am proud to have made for him. I don't know what his doctor did with his foreskin. I tell my friends that I was able to keep it and I planted it in the backyard and come spring we are going to have a lovely penis tree.

At the time of the circumcision, often when I brought up the upcoming agenda in mixed company, I was berated and called barbaric. Those parents can kiss my ass. And while they are down there they can look around for my foreskin because it ain't there. I don't miss my foreskin. I am thrilled to be circumcised. I never think about what might have been. I don't have any feelings of loss over the foreskin I was born with being in a medical bag somewhere on a barge in the Atlantic Ocean. I've never had a woman pull down my pants and say "Ew." I take pride in my pink fireman's cap. I like the way my penis looks and I really like to use it, so I don't see how traumatic the circumcision could have been. You would think that if it were such a traumatic experience, guys would be a little gun-shy about letting other people touch their dicks. This isn't the case. In fact, the opposite is true. It's almost as if being circumcised liberated us all from feeling shame about our privates and we can't wait to share them with the rest of the world.

If you are reading this and you are not circumcised, I am not saying your parents did anything wrong or that I think any less of you. In fact, I think more of you . . . about a quarter of an inch more of you. But I cannot urge you enough to circumcise your child. God forbid if you let your uncircumcised child change for gym class and get caught with his pants down by a bully.

It is because of kids' cruelty that I also encourage all parents to teach their child some type of self-defense. I wish my father had taught me how to defend myself. I would come home from school and tell him that a bully kept shoving me around and punching me and all he said was "Go tell a teacher." Bad idea, Dad. We all know that telling a teacher on a bully is school suicide. It took twice the amount of balls to rat someone out as it did to stand up for yourself and punch them in the chops.

This is why I'm thrilled that Jackie loves karate and is good at it. I plan to also put him in jujitsu, kung fu, tae kwon do, boxing, and Pilates. Hell, I even started taking kung fu myself shortly before he was born. I don't care about the art of it or the Zen and Tao of self-defense. I just don't ever want to get beat up in front of my kid. That's a tough one to come back from.

We all have an earliest memory, whether it's the curtains in your nursery, the sound of your mother's voice, or a tree in your yard. I am going to be damn sure that my son's first lasting memory isn't one of me lying on the ground crying louder than he is after getting my teeth kicked in. Can you imagine getting beat up in front of your kid? What if that is his first memory? Years and years go by and as he enters his teens, the two of you begin to have a little power struggle. One afternoon, you have enough and you yell, "Get in this house and clean your room or I am going to kick your ass!" How mortifying to have your son slowly look up and calmly say, "Oh, *today* you're a man? I remember when I was two and you got beat down like a little bitch when we were walking through Long Beach!" Ouch.

As fathers, we all have masculine dreams for our sons. We want our boys to be tough and not take any shit from anyone, no matter what. The truth is, if our sons learn to play the violin and walk with a little sashay in their hips, we will love them as much as ever. We won't be able to help ourselves. How can you turn your back on God?

I'd be lying if I said I never asked myself, What if my son is gay? At one time or another, every father has asked himself this. Hopefully not while watching his son dressed head to toe as Barbra Streisand, stepping into a Miata. It's a good question to ask yourself, if for no other reason than to come to grips with the fact that if your son is gay, it happened long before you got your mitts on him. The big question, in my opinion: How can I facilitate my son's gayness in the right direction? Because I'll tell you right now that if Jackie were gay, Nik and I would help him become the coolest, most badass gay dude that ever skipped around the planet. My gay kid wouldn't be some chubby, two-bit hustler acting catty toward everyone he meets. No, our son would be *fabulous*.

He'd still be enrolled in karate to avoid the ass-kicking. No son of mine is ever going to be beat up for being gay. If another kid wants to fight my son because he is acting like an asshole, he can be my guest. But if you plan on being a "fag basher," prepare to die a slow, painful, gay death. Nik and I would be sure that our kid was listening to plenty of Rufus Wainwright and reading lots of Oscar Wilde. We would style him and be sure he was erudite and strong and could sing the Rodgers and Hammerstein catalog as well as throw chop blocks and sweeps.

I have not only wondered if Jackie was gay, I've also sometimes wondered if I'm gay. I can say with some confidence that many men have this flash in their heads at some point in their lives. Hopefully not while at the bottom of a pile of men you have met at a rest area on the Garden State Parkway. I have asked myself this question more and more of late. You see, I recently had a couple of corporate shows to do in Las Vegas and I had a few days of downtime between gigs. Nik and I were browsing the local entertainment magazines looking for cool shows to go see. I was reading *VEGAS,* when I came across an ad for the Liberace Museum. As soon as I saw the words *Liberace Museum,* I felt a tractor beam pulling me toward the address on the ad.

So off we went to the Liberace Museum in the middle of the steaming-hot Vegas day. The moment I walked into the place, I became fascinated with Liberace. Before that day, I never thought about him at all except when I saw the Bugs Bunny episode when Bugs does an impression of him: "I wish my brother George was here." Now, as I walked the fur-lined hallways of the exhibit, I was convinced that no greater entertainer has ever lived.

I bought everything in the gift shop—Liberace snow globes, T-shirts, and a bowling ball bag with Lee's face on it. The next evening, we had the pleasure of seeing Bette Midler perform at Caesars Palace. At one point during "Wind Beneath My Wings," I freaking cried. It was inspiring! The following night was a Sunday and the little lady and I decided to stay in, order room service, and watch the Oscars. We sat Indian-style on the floor and picked at our Cobb salads while judging all the stars' outfits.

Two nights later I was in Manhattan for another corporate show. I asked the concierge at the hotel to get me a couple of Knicks tickets for a Wednesday night game at the Garden. I was so pumped to go see my beloved Knickerbockers. I hadn't been to Madison Square Garden since the team was actually good. That was when I was in my twenties. Now, at forty, I was going to bring my beloved bride to my old stomping grounds. Except this time I wouldn't have nosebleed seats. Nope, this time, like a conquering hetero hero, I would march my superhot wife right down to the front row and watch the entire game with my toes courtside.

Well, a funny thing happened on the way to the Garden. I was reading *Time Out New York* and came across an ad for Liza Minnelli at the Palace. Suddenly the Knicks were irrelevant. We *had* to go see Liza's show, no? Liza is getting old. What if we get to go to the show where she slips and falls? That would be awesome. (Not Liza Minnelli falling but having the privilege to be at the show where Liza Minnelli fell down because she was too old to perform, of course.) I called down to the concierge and giddily asked them to secure me some Liza tickets. They called back a few minutes later and said that I had great seats for Liza and the cost would be . . . aww, who cares what cost? I would have spent double whatever it is, for crying out loud! We're talking about freaking Liza! What if she falls?!

I canceled the Knicks and told my wife that we were going to see Liza freakin' Minnelli instead. She was happy about it and we went to the Palace theater and took our seats. As we waited for the curtain to rise, a woman kneeled in the aisle next to us and said, "Hi, Jay, Nik. Liza is so excited you guys are here tonight. She would love it if you could come backstage after the show to say hi."

I almost crapped my pants. I have never been a huge fan of show tunes or Broadway, in particular, but I knew enough about it to know that seeing and meeting Liza Minnelli is about as common as meeting Derek Jeter, and Derek Jeter don't sing. We promptly agreed to meet Liza and then spent the entire performance nervous about it. I remember she sang "New York, New York" but other than that, I'm not sure what happened. Nik and I both just sat there with a case of the sweats, feeling like we were going to throw up. What would we say? What would we do once we said what we said? How long are we supposed to stay? What if she wants us to swing with her? Too many questions were flying through my head to enjoy the show.

Finally, after the encore, the woman appeared again and escorted us through the crowd to Liza Minnelli's dressing room.

Within seconds we were sitting on little couches with Liza as she told us how great *we* were for about fifteen minutes. We were completely starstruck. This woman has an Oscar. This woman is a legend. This woman is listening to everything I say. I have to tell you that Liza Minnelli is a very attractive woman. She is more attractive in person than the camera has ever given her credit for. She is also one of the nicest people that God has put on this earth. I assure you, this woman is one of the true greats.

Adding to the bizarreness of it all, we all wound up exchanging numbers and giving each other big hugs good-bye. Liza signed my *Playbill.* She wrote "To Jay and Nik, my newest babies! I was both flabbed and gasted to have met you both! All my love, LIZA."

I skipped home. What an event! I felt so lucky to be in the greatest city in the world with the most amazing woman in the world and have become friends with one of the biggest entertainers in the world. I thought about the week I had just had. And that's when I realized that I am gay. I mean, *really* gay. I just pulled a random week out of my life and what did I do with it? How did I spend my crazy, wacky life on the road? I saw Liza Minnelli. I cried at Bette Midler. I watched the Oscars (I always watch the Oscars, but somehow watching the Oscars while eating a Cobb salad made the activity very gay), I saw Liza Minnelli. I met Liza Minnelli. I got Liza Minnelli's autograph. The only thing that could make my week any gayer is if I were actually juggling dicks in my spare time . . . with my face and ass. Then and only then could I have spent a gayer week in my life. The odd thing about it all is that my wife didn't cajole me into any of it. *It was all my idea.* Gay.

We flew back to Los Angeles the next day and on the flight home I gave the pilot a hand job in the bathroom.

Okay, I made that part up, but the rest of it is true.

When we got home, Nik and I went to pick Jackie up at school. Every day, when we do this, he gets into the car and after we all give kisses and hugs, I ask, "What did you do in school today, pal?" and every day, his answer is always a well-thought-out, "Um, I don't know." Every freaking day I ask this boy what he did in school that day and every motherfreaking day he says, "Um, I don't know." Since the private school we send him to has the same yearly tuition as Syracuse (not kidding), I would like to know what happens behind its walls after I drop my kid off in the morning.

Jackie's preschool was a pretty hippy-dippy "how are we all feeling today?" type of affair. The teachers there were all wonderful educators, though, and the school was fantastic for three- and four-year-olds. The preschool's policy on parent or friend visitation: whenever you want, come on by and stay as long as you like! That was a big selling point at the time. When you finally let your baby bird out of the nest you definitely want a school that will let you watch him learn to fly. Since it was a preschool, the academic schedule was routine and rudimentary. The kids finger-painted and dressed up and played with blocks and Big Wheels. That was my son's domain at preschool for three years. He was ruler of the Big Wheels. They were very important to him. Every time I would pick him up from school, he would be tearing up the schoolyard on a Big Wheel. It was great to see him playing so free of self-consciousness, though at the same time, for fifteen thousand dollars a year, I thought maybe the school should have had him learning to speak Japanese. Nope. Just Big Wheels. Fifteen g's a year and my little guy rides a Big Wheel for three hours a day. If the SATs have a three-wheeler section, my son is going to Harvard.

Jackie's new elementary school is incredible. It is already worth every penny. They have exceptional educators and we are lucky he was accepted there. The school has a slightly stricter policy on parent visitation than his previous school did and with the move to this school, I was excited to learn what my son was doing each day. The big stumbling block to this was that, for some reason, he could never remember.

Children have astounding and mysterious memories. They are very selective and have the ability to not remember traumatic things that may have happened to them in years past or remember the most mundane detail of life from three years prior and obsess over it for weeks on end. My son obviously doesn't remember being in the neonatal intensive care unit, nor does he remember his third birthday party. However, Jackie could tell you in spectacular detail about the time I stepped in dog shit while buying our Christmas tree when he was two and a half.

Yet here we are again, every day: "What did you learn in school today?"

And every day: "Um, I don't know."

Finally, on this one day, I told Jackie that this dialogue (I'm being generous) was no longer okay. If I am going to pay for one of the best private schools in the country to educate my son, one of the things that they can teach him is to tell his father what he learned in the course of a day. I told Jackie that from now on, he had to remember one thing he learned that day. That was all I was asking. One thing that he learned. I don't need a lesson plan or anything but I would like some proof that he was actually there. He agreed to this and we shook on it.

The next day, Nik and I picked Jackie up from school and he climbed into the truck and said nothing. Finally I asked him if he remembered our deal. He told me he did and then he squinted real tightly to help him concentrate. Eventually he said, "Daddy, I really tried to remember one thing I learned today but I can't think of anything."

I told him to think some more. He closed his eyes again. After a few beats, he looked up and said flatly, "I can't. I'm sorry, Daddy."

I began to worry that Jackie was the world's youngest Alzheimer's patient. Then I thought, Is he smoking grass? He has no medical problems and his only head injury was the minor soccer incident; maybe he can't remember anything because he smokes an eighth a week behind my back. No wonder he wants privacy all of a sudden during bathtime—he has hollowed out his SpongeBob raft and turned it into a bong!

I didn't want Jackie to think I was mad at him for forgetting, though, so I said, "Okay, instead of telling me something you *learned* today, maybe you can tell me something you *did* today. Not something you learned, just something you did. You can name anything. Anything you did at all is fair game. Just tell me something."

Jackie thought for a second and then said, "Okay! I can tell you something I learned today, Daddy!"

I was relieved, to say the least. I said, "Okay, pal, tell me, what is the one thing you did in school today that you remember?"

"I played Kissy Boy."

"Um, Kissy Boy?"

Jackie smiled a big grin and said, "Yeah! Kissy Boy. It's extreme!"

"Son, what is Kissy B—"

Jackie couldn't wait to be asked; he jumped all over it. He shouted, "In Kissy Boy, all the boys run around like we are playing tag but instead of tagging the man, you have to give him a kiss!"

I was a little speechless. More than twenty thousand dollars a year now and my son is learning how to act like Andy Dick on Fire Island. I asked my son, "Do you ever play Kissy Boy with *girls*?"

"No, Daddy. That would be gross," he said, matter-of-factly. So that was the answer that I waited months for. Kissy Boy. My son said nothing about the fact that he is learning to read. He never told me that he was going to be taught how to count and add with dollars and coins. He didn't tell me that he knows more Spanish than I do. Jackie never explained that he loves science and he often asks his teacher if smoke could reach Mars and that once when he was told no, he asked, "What could we do to help smoke reach Mars? Can you safely keep smoke inside of a rocket with men inside?"

No. My son mentioned none of that. My son told me that at school he remembers playing Kissy Boy. Be careful what you wish for. All I wanted was one answer. Kissy Boy.

I let Jackie off the hook. I wasn't going to break his chops about Kissy Boy. If he wanted to spend time at one of the finest schools in the country kissing boys on the run, who was I to tell him that wasn't okay? To be fair, I have never even played Kissy Boy. Maybe it's fun.

That night, I lay in bed and wondered, Is Jackie gay? If he is, I hope he knows that I think it's fine and I love him unconditionally. This really weighed heavily on my mind as I lay there in the dark. What if my kid is gay? What if my kid is gay? Then I rolled over and caught a glimpse of the signed Liza Minnelli *Playbill* on my nightstand. Next to it was a Liberace coaster holding a bottle of Perrier. I had what the Buddhists call clarity. My son plays Kissy Boy but I am an absolute fag.

15

STEPPARENTING SUCKS

How can I put this gently without offending any of you fine readers? Being a stepparent sucks. Screw this "happily blended family" shit. The Brady Bunch can blow me. And to hell with anyone who says "There is no difference." That is a lie. There *is* a difference. A huge, glaring every-two-weeks-my-son-isn't-with-me difference. The difference between being a parent and a stepparent is a delicate one.

When you are a stepparent, no matter how hard and completely you love your child, you always come in last place. I say this from a fortunate perspective. Jackie met Nik when he was still in diapers and could barely form words. His entire memory bank includes his "Peey guhl." He knows no life before her. She has always been a steady, loving presence in his life. He never met any "dates" of mine. There were never any skanks walking through the house during breakfast. There were never any strange women sitting with him and me having uncomfortable "family" meals at Sizzler filled with forced laughter and too many trips to the salad bar to escape the tension. Jackson has the incredible benefit of never having to ask me "Whatever happened to what's her name?"

From the moment Nik and I met, the three of us were indeed a family. But here is the secret, terrible message to all the good stepparents out there. When you really love a child as if he came out of your own DNA, they break your heart just as often and with as little remorse as they do their biological parents. Sadly, and completely unfairly, because you have the word *step* before your name, you always feel lesser than.

Stepparents cannot discipline with impunity. Stepparents cannot reference their kids without some dismissive asshole hearing the word *step* and tuning them out. Through the media and a large part of society we have seen the stepparent portrayed as cold, distant, evil, cruel, spiteful, and downright hateful. Cinderella, anyone? Sometimes this portrayal is sadly accurate. But thank the good Lord above that there are also incredible stepparents out there. Stepkids may have it just as bad. In the best-run households, children must feel such confusion. They love and trust parents *and* stepparents. How can they possibly love them all without feeling like they are betraying someone? However, it can be done. Many of you holding this book are constantly busting your ass each and every day to prove to your stepchildren that you *do* love them. More so that you love them completely and unconditionally.

One morning I was eavesdropping on Nik and Jackie having one of their long, silly, unimportant and vitally important talks. Nik was getting Jackie ready for school just as she does every morning at five. She sets her alarm to get up before him so that when he wakes up he never feels alone. He always knows she is downstairs. She is always making muffins or biscuits or chocolate milk or writing his napkin note for his lunchbox. In short, she makes sure that when he wakes up, he knows that there is always a parent awake, getting the house just right and taking care of everything. Our Pretty Girl is the best at taking care of everything.

I overheard Jackie say to Nik, "I don't know why people say 'step' when they are talking about parents and kids." Then he dropped some awesome kid logic. "I mean, all it is is who you married first."

Nik was quiet for a second and I could tell by the length of her silence that she was fighting back tears. "Well," she said, "I know we don't feel any 'step' in *our* family. I just feel lucky that I get to be one of your three parents—that Daddy and Mommy and I are all on the same team. Team *you!*" (Note to the reader. Nik actually said that. This isn't just some Dr. Phil crap that I copied and pasted.) After the "team you" speech, Jackson was quiet for a few moments. (He wasn't trying not to cry; he had accidentally put both of his legs through the same leg hole on his pants.) Finally he looked at Nik and said, "I really don't like the 'step' part. I'm going to call you Momma Nik because you *are* a mommy." He turned back to his pants. I turned into a bowl of emotional pudding.

Nik calmly walked downstairs and pulled a pound cake out of the oven. When she set it down on the counter, she was a mother.

Jackson has always felt very strongly about Nik. When he was three and he was sleeping in a crib, he would not go to sleep until his pretty girl came in to kiss him goodnight. She would always get down on the carpet and say, "Give me those wips [lips]!" Jackie would then roll over on his side and push his pursed lips through the bars of the crib and they would have a smooch good night. One night Jackie asked Nik if she had any kids that were hers. She told him no. He then asked why not. She explained, "I'm just not a mommy yet."

My son reached his skinny arms through the wooden crib bars, held Momma Nik's face in his hands, and said firmly, "You are a mommy!"

That time she cried.

So you see, stepparenting, like parenting, can be a shit job. Even when it is done right and you have given all that your heart can carry to a child, he can still break it just the same as if you gave birth to him. I agree with Jackie when he says, "I don't know why people say 'step.' " Sometimes the word *step* really does mean nothing. Many of you stepparents out there have known your "stepchildren" since they were babies. These children don't have any memories without you in them. There was never a time in your daughter's life when you didn't put her needs ahead of your own. There is a stigma that is unfairly attached to the word *step*. And I suppose that the stepparent is the one person in the post-divorce dynamic that can most put a monkey wrench into a child's future. But the good ones don't. Good stepparents have one of the strangest and most difficult jobs in parenting. They are the ones that have to shift through endless, thoughtful hours with their stepchild before they can prove that it is also their job to make everything all right. Each early morning and each late night with this child puts his mind more at ease. Each day the child feels safer and safer and less like he is betraying someone by having true feelings of love and affection for this other parent.

I would like to take this page in the book to take my hat off to all the good stepparents out there who are dispelling the Evil Stepmom and Stepdad Myth. You are making a difference.

....

16

THE BIRDS AND THE BEES

When are we supposed to tell our children about the birds and the bees? Obviously the answer is different with each child but if you had to pick an age, what would you say was right? Seven? Eight? If you guessed anything under six, Chris Hansen is walking through your front door right now. Jackie and I almost had the talk when he was six. Almost. The tub was running and he was getting undressed for his bath.

He looked at me and asked, "Daddy, what are balls for?"

I told him that balls are what make boys different from girls. We have balls and they don't. I also told him that they are also called testicles.

Jackie was now naked and able to hold his balls in his hand to use them as an example. He asked, "But what do testicleballs do?"

I was not prepared for this conversation. I said, "Let me think about it for a second."

"What are they for? What are testicleballs' job in the body?"

Damn. I spoke slowly and deliberately, trying to feel my way through the right way to explain testicleballs to my son. I told him, "Well, Jackie, you know that men are men, right? And women are women. We have balls and they have vaginas."

"I know."

I was both relieved and angered at the same time. I was glad I wasn't going to have to explain to my son what a vagina is, but at the same time, how the hell did my son know what a vagina was?!

"Daddy, I know a heart pumps blood. I know my lungs are for breathing. Why do we have balls?"

I told him that when a man and woman have a baby together, the balls help make the baby. I wanted to smoke-screen that as quickly as possible, so I immediately added, "When you get whiskers and hair on your chest, that is because of your balls, too."

Jackie was now in the tub and his balls were thankfully covered by bubbles so neither of us could see them. (That would have made everything a little more uncomfortable.)

"What is the balls' job in the body?"

Jeez, this kid was relentless. I swallowed and said, "They help make babies." I braced for his next question, which I was sure was going to be "How do balls help make babies?"

In an act of mercy, my son's next sentence was, "Oh."

And we were done. He began playing with toy sharks and army men in the tub and all ball talk was officially finished. In hindsight, it was pretty cool. I am fairly certain that my son was not ready to hear about how testicleballs work, so he dropped it. Personally, I didn't think he was ready to know how a baby is made. I am just not prepared to have my kid walking around first grade with that knowledge. He is so damned competitive; I can see him saying to a friend, "I bet you don't even know how a baby is made!" Then for the next hour at recess he could hold court and introduce vaginas and the proper use of testicleballs to the entire first grade. I would then be called in and Jackie would be expelled and it would all be because I gave him "the talk" a little too early.

I remember when I officially learned about the birds and the bees—when my mother explained the exact workings of the male and female parts. We were in her car at the corner of Bradford and Pompton avenues in Cedar Grove, New Jersey. I am not sure what prompted the conversation but I was eight and I had, up until that point, been operating on false street knowledge, so as I coolly listened to my mother talk about vaginas and penises, I acted like I already knew. Secretly I was incredibly relieved. My friends and I had figured out the birds and the bees long ago and often spoke about it freely. Every kid on Valley View Road knew that in order to make a baby you had to pee in someone's butt. Yes, that is what we thought. Up until that moment in my mother's car, I was horrified at the thought that I was made by my father taking a leak in my mother's ass. Furthermore, I was deathly afraid of having to pee in someone's butt when I got older. Subsequently, as my mother gave me "the talk," I felt an enormous weight lifted off my shoulders.

Nik had a completely different experience with "the talk" when she was a little girl. At the age of four, having no knowledge of how a baby is made at all, she simply asked her mother. Her mother then very matter-of-factly explained how a penis goes inside a vagina until the man ejaculates. Nik's first question when her mom was finished talking was "Does it feel good?" Wow. I really got off easy with Jackie. I cannot possibly conceive of a four-year-old girl asking me "Does it feel good?" My knee-jerk response to protect my baby girl would have been to say *"No! It's dirty and it hurts!"* I guess that's why God made it so Terry got Nik, Jeannie got J.J., and J.J. got Jackie.

But Nik didn't even stop at "Does it feel good?" She went on to ask, "Does Daddy lay on top of you or do you sit on his lap?" And also, "Can you do it standing up?" Terry Cox very calmly explained all the ways and varieties that sex can be performed to make a baby. She never flinched. She is a better man than I. She and Nik laugh when they retell this story. I laugh along with them but secretly I am planning to teach my daughter great shame the first time she brings up sex.

These are three different scenarios from three different decades asking about sex. It just goes to show you how each child is so vastly different from the other. Some kids walk around at four knowing every position you can have sex in. Other kids are seven years old and think that the way to make a baby is to pee in someone's ass. Other kids just aren't quite ready to have "the talk" yet. I hope you, dear reader, have timed your child properly. Personally, I think it would be hilarious if someone taught their child that to get someone pregnant you have to pee in her ass. Hold on a second; Chris Hansen just walked into my house.

17

MY LOUSY SWIMMERS

I am not sure how many men have written this before but if I am the first, so be it. My sperm count absolutely sucks. When Nik and I went to a fertility doctor to get my sperm counted, the test came back that I had none—twice. This seemed impossible considering that I had already made one kid with my sperm. I found it hard to believe that in six years, the few remaining sperm I had left were already retired. Regardless, something wasn't right. No matter how hard Nik and I tried (and believe me, we were trying hard), she wasn't getting pregnant. My bride had been to her gynecologist regularly and the OB-GYN tested her for all types of problems that may arise down the road en route to a normal, healthy pregnancy. She had a great uterus and all signs pointed to her body as a perfect place to house a fetus for nine months. The doctor also checked on the quality of her eggs. This was the only time I have ever been allowed in the room during a gynecological exam. Ladies, on behalf of all men, let me say "I'm sorry."

I had no idea how awful a trip to the gynecologist can be for a woman. Apparently the vagina is a very complicated place and women see their special vagina doctor twice a year for maintenance. This baffles me. Guys have it so much easier. There is no penis doctor. There is no cocktologist. If it burns when we pee, we go see someone. (So far, so good.) Women don't have it so easy. So many things can go wrong with a vagina. When you hear all the parts involved, it is almost like going to a mechanic. There are outer and inner labia. There are hoods and gaskets and manifolds and ovaries and lots of tubes. Things are measured and compared to prior measurements. Most shocking to me is that there are actual tools involved. Women lie down on an examining table and have to put their feet up into cold metal stirrups. If your wife's doctor is very kind, like mine, they will cover the stirrups with little pot holders. *Pot holders.* That is where we are in medicine in this century. We put pot holders over stirrups to keep our feet warm! Why not hand puppets while we're at it? Have a chicken or a lion staring down into the spot.

The stirrups aren't close together, either. They are spread far apart and your wife lies there, helplessly spread-eagled, waiting for the doctor to enter the room. Sometimes while they are lying spread-eagled, a nurse will come into the room to check a chart or move some apparatus. Sometimes the nurse is a man. Sometimes the doctor will have medical students with him and ask your wife if it is okay if they audit the class for the day. In this case, the class is your wife's box. Each visit, our lovely ladies lie there and suffer through this humiliation. Let's be honest: if men had to go through a similar visit every six months we wouldn't show up. Subsequently, our private parts would be a mess. You would pull down our pants and see a true abomination of neglect. If you don't believe me, ask your husband when he last had his teeth cleaned. Yikes. We can't even take care of the parts of our body that are showing. There would be flies and old school photos stuck in spiderwebs stuck to our pubes. You would pull down our pants and bats would fly out. Our balls would be sandwiched between old gum wrappers and empty toilet paper rolls.

Women go to these appointments without complaining and then, miraculously, come home and actually groom and landscape the *outside*. Again, on behalf of all men—ladies, thank you.

So, Nik was lying spread-eagled on the gynecologist's table with her feet in the cold stirrups while we waited for the doctor to come in. It's odd how little small talk you can generate when your wife is laid out like a sex offering for a Saudi prince. Finally the doctor comes in and before she finishes her hello, she is squirting an enormous amount of lube jelly into her gloved hand. Usually, when you or I have used lube in our lives, we have used an amount that was about the size of a quarter. But the gynecologist just keeps squeezing the bottle of lube until there is a snowball-sized mountain of lube in her palm. The OB-GYN is completely unfazed by your wife's glory spread to the world. It is the most normal part of her day. In fact, OB-GYNs seem to be experts at small talk while inserting and retrieving things from our wives' vaginas. I didn't know if I was supposed to break it up or say words of encouragement. Considering my wife had been seeing a gynecologist regularly for eighteen years, I decided she probably knows what she's doing and to keep my mouth shut. The doctor put more lube on her hands and fingers and put some horrible-looking instruments into Nik. I wondered if I was somehow crossing a pervert line by holding Nik's hand during all of this.

Mostly I was filled with the knowledge that my presence was completely unnecessary. I knew nothing. I definitely had no idea how many times a gynecologist can say the words "slide down" or "move lower." Forty-three. That is how many times on average your wife's gynecologist will say these words. It's absurd. Eventually your wife will have her ass hanging over the edge of the table and her knees will be against her ears. After more lube is put in her, the doctor lubes pretty much everything in the room. A golfball-sized amount is squeezed out onto what looks like a metal duck. The bill of the duck goes where you may guess. It looks like a medieval torture device. In a way, it could be because once the metal duck is inside your wife, the doctor winds it open. *What the fuck is going on here?* It's like the vagina is on the rack and the doctor keeps winding and winding until the vagina breaks down and confesses. "Okay, stop! I confess! I slept with a Puerto Rican guy in college!"

The metal duck gets put away and the doctor replaces it with a few oversized Q-tips and more cold metal instruments. Everything is cold at the gynecologist's office. They even warn you before they put it inside you. Hey, doctors, why not just warm everything up *before* the little lady lies down spread-eagled? That would be more humane.

The doctor put a camera inside Nik to see how her eggs looked. It was like a two-man Easter egg hunt with a monitor. As the OB-GYN rolled a camera from side to side inside Nik, the three of us looked up toward a television screen that was broadcasting Nik's insides. There were no commercials. There was just an endless loop of my wife's beautiful eggs. There seemed to be thousands of them! It looked a bit like when they pull Ping-Pong balls out of those huge containers for the lottery on the news. There were so many eggs and the doctor told us they were all perfect for conception. The Vag Cam also showed that my Nik did not have a "hostile uterus." I didn't know that this term even existed. What exactly is a "hostile uterus"? Does the fertilized egg get hazed? Does the uterus drink too much and yell at the eggs? Regardless, my wife, reproduction-wise, was perfect. (She's perfect in other ways, too.) That meant that everyone in the room immediately knew that the reason we weren't getting pregnant lay within me. More accurately, the reason we weren't getting pregnant was what didn't lie within me.

I was born two months premature in 1970. Due to my early birth, some of my organs needed more time to develop. (But I dunked in the third grade! And I'm *huge!*) As a kid, my lungs were always a problem. I had bronchitis three times a year. My bladder is still too small and I wake up many times each night to empty it. Also due to my premature birth, my balls had not fallen into my ball bag when I was born. We know now that in time, testicles eventually drop into the sack naturally, but in 1970 the doctors thought it would be a good idea to sew my testicles to the sides of my thighs. My tiny balls were up somewhere near my stomach and the doctor thought it wise to stitch rubber bands around them and attach the other end of the rubber band to my legs. The theory was that each time I would kick my legs like a baby does, I would forcibly yank my tiny balls down into their pouch. My father still shivers when I bring this up. Forty years later, and he nearly vomits at the memory of my balls being yanked from point A to point B. He has told me that for over a month he could not be in the same room as my crib because of the Nazi-like experiment that was happening in my onesie. It will come as no surprise to you that this method of forcing balls to drop is very bad, in the long run, for generating sperm. In short, it creates hostile testicles.

After the testing and retesting of Nik's reproductive powers, it was my turn to check to see if my parts were working.

I knew I would not have to go through nearly as much as Nik did. I wouldn't have to lie down in stirrups and watch the Vag Cam. I didn't think I would even need any lube. My instructions were simple: go to a fertility doctor's office and masturbate into a cup. After I masturbated into a cup, the fertility doctor would count how many sperm I had each time I ejaculated. He would also tell me if the sperm were mobile and had good motility. I am not sure what *motility* means but after you are told to masturbate into a cup you sort of tune the rest of the sentence out.

I began to think of what a strange job it is to be a fertility doctor. You deal with other guys' jiz all day, every day. How do you get into that line of work? Are you a junior in college and you have an epiphany? "I really love to be around semen!" "I am always happy when I am working with it! If I could get a job handling cum, it wouldn't be like working at all!"

I'm just curious as to how one decides on that particular specialty within his medical degree. Some ground rules for my sperm sample were laid out. I was vaguely familiar with these ground rules because seven years ago I gave a sperm sample to make Jackson. He was a test-tube baby. I used in vitro fertilization. They took the best-looking sperm I had and they placed it inside the best egg they could find and Jackie happened.

The ground rules are simple: no ejaculation for five days prior to giving your sperm sample. Wow, that's a long time. I happen to have a smokin' hot wife, so the thought of not putting the mail in the mailbox for five days is a bit daunting. It's not

247

like porn, where I can just put her away. We sleep in the same bed and I often see her naked. Five days is a long time. When I was much younger and gave a sperm sample, five days of abstinence was also nearly impossible. I was a chronic masturbator. I rubbed one out at least once a day, like most teenagers. I would daydream about how I would masturbate if I found myself in difficult situations. Like how would I masturbate in the army? I would have to learn to do it without moving a muscle or the bunk bed. What if I was in a full body cast? I would starve myself until I was super skinny inside my body cast and turn my back to the window. I would have spinal tap holes in the back and sides of my body cast. I would let the sunlight come through the window and angle it into the spinal tap holes. Then I would get an erection and try to angle the tip of my penis into the incoming sunbeam. Then I would hit my morphine button five times in a row and make love to the sun. What? You never thought of this? I guess that is what separates the masturbators from the chronic masturbators.

So I didn't ejaculate for five days. On the sixth day, I drove to the doctor's office to put my dolphins in the tank. Be advised. Don't make the same mistake I made. I was wearing corduroy pants with no underwear. Walking through the parking garage, because of the friction, I was lucky I made it to the front door! I had to John Wayne my way through the building to avoid an accident in my ribbed pants.

Once in the doctor's office, a nurse handed me a cup and

asked if I was ready. I wasn't sure what she meant. Did she think I needed to warm up? Stretch? It's been nearly a week. Let's go! She showed me into a room and told me there were magazines and DVDs in case I needed help. Good to know. Then as she left, she said, "Don't forget to lock the door." Yeah, check. Call me conservative but usually I lock the door when I am jerking off on the floor of the doctor's office trying to arc semen into a cup. I am going to lock the door. I am going to lock the door, chain the door, and slide the bookshelf in front of the door. I am going to dig a goddamn tiger pit in front of the door. I have few rules that I live by but at that moment the big one I had was that *no one* was going to walk in on me jacking off at the doctor's office. Did they think I would forget to lock the door? Did they think I was going to leave it ajar in case someone I knew walked by and I wanted to shout a quick hello? I was already on my way to locking the door when the nurse told me to remember to lock the door!

I found myself alone in a room at the doctor's office and all I had to do was begin masturbating into a cup. I looked at the cup and thought about the five days I had not ejaculated. I thought that I might need a bigger cup. I thought of the Gatorade bottle I had in my truck. After not fooling around for five days I was unsure of what would happen when I was finally able to let loose. I figured I could take graffiti off a brick wall after abstaining for five days. I could break up a protest. You get the idea. I started to look around for all of the porn the nurse had told me about. I opened one of the drawers in a small cabinet and there was the mother lode of porn collections. The doctor had such incredible titles such as *Anal Assassins, Say Ahhhh, Schindler's Fist,* and my personal favorite, *Total Anal Destruction*. I had not yet seen *Total Anal Destruction* but I doubted it was going to be as good as the book. I also noticed that all of these movies had all-male casts. I wasn't prepared for that curveball. The nurse told me there were magazines and movies to help me. She didn't mention that all the porn provided was *gay porn*. Now what do I do? I could give *Say Aaaaah* a try but what if I liked it? Then suddenly I would have to redo a lot of paperwork in my brain. I decided to skip the porn and instead concentrate on a loving kiss that Nik gave me before I walked into the room. It worked. Four seconds later, my cup almost runneth over. The problem now was that no one told me what to do next. I had been given instructions to masturbate into a cup. No one said what to do when I was finished. So I just sat there for a while, waiting to see if anyone would come around and knock. They didn't. After about ten minutes of waiting, I mustered up the courage to walk out into the hallway and try to track down the nurse. I was still wearing my hospital gown; I was sweating and still had half a boner. I looked like a maniac. I meekly tiptoed into the hallway and looked around. There was one other guy in the hallway with his cup of semen and half a boner and neither of us was too eager to make eye contact.

Finally the nurse reappeared and took the cup out of my hands. She asked, "Was it a completed ejaculate?" I had no idea

what this meant. I asked her to repeat the question. Mildly annoyed, she asked again, "Was it a completed ejaculate? It's a
standard question." I had to confess, "I have no idea what that
means." She leaned closer and said, "Did it all get in the cup?"
What the hell kind of question is that? Of course it all got in the
cup! I'm there to put it all in the cup! Why would she ask me
this? Did someone miss one day? They must have made a hell of
a mess for it to have become a standard question once you leave
the masturbation station. Maybe one day a janitor walked out
of the room with a mop over his shoulder and yelled out, "No
more! That is the last time! It looked like spin art! From now
on you ask them if it was a completed ejaculate!" How would
someone miss? Didn't they stretch? Did one day a guy set the
cup up on the radiator and said, "Check this out, through the
ceiling fan, off the wall, nothing but cup." Were a few guys playing horse? Regardless of why, it was now a standard question. I
wanted to tell her that I put some in one of the drawers for shits
and giggles but instead I just said, "Yes."

My work was now finished. Next the fertility doctor would
put my semen under a microscope and count my sperm. My
answer came in the mail from some futuristic-sounding laboratory. The document basically said that there was no evidence of
sperm in my sample. I was devastated. Nik was devastated. This
was shocking news. It is shocking to be told that basically, if
you want to have a baby, you better send away for one and have
it mailed back to you. I felt so lousy. Poor Nik, whose biggest,

brightest dream in life was to raise children, wouldn't be able to carry mine. I felt useless.

I gave another sample a week later to see if there might have been an error. Same result. I decided to visit the fertility doctor whom I used seven years ago when Jackson was born. This man had already counted my sperm personally and maybe he would give me a different diagnosis than the current doctor. The older we get, the more we do this. We will go see different doctors until we find one who tells us what we want to hear. Things like "You should be able to get back to your basketball league a few days after your knee surgery" or "Yes, you do need a prescription for Vicodin."

Again I was to masturbate into a cup and again the majority of the porn was gay. (What *is* up with that?) When I finished, Nik and I walked into the doctor's office. He took my semen sample and transferred some of it onto a slide and looked at it under a microscope. We sat there holding our breath. There was a computer monitor on his desk showing what was on the slide. While he was looking at my sample and moving the slide around, the monitor looked like a snowstorm. Nothing but white, blank space filled the screen. I hung my head. I heard the doctor say, "Here's one!" Men are supposed to have 20 million sperm per ejaculate and here I was in an office in Westwood hearing a doctor yell out, "Here's one." *One?* What if that was my good one? I panicked thinking that my left-handed reliever or my middle linebacker of a son was lying on the doctor's slide under a microscope. We knew I didn't have many, so let's not waste the ones we find. The doctor then said, "Here's another one" and then, "This guy is no good."

He found a couple more "good guys" after that. It was incredible news. I had sperm. They were just a small, ragtag bunch of misfits like the cast of *Red Dawn*. It turns out that the problem I have is that my sperm do not come out all the way from my body. They either stay in my balls or die a slow death in my urethra. I had very little sperm but the doctor was positive that he could extract a bunch and use them with Nik's eggs. I immediately asked, "How do you extract them?" The doctor then went on to explain how he would have me lie down with my feet up in stirrups and put me under. He would cut open my testicles and remove each individual sperm that looked viable. Then he would sew my ball sack back up. I was speechless and fighting the urge to run for the hills. The guy was going to slice me open like an apple, pick out the seeds, and put the apple back together. It sounded so horrifying, but after being told I had nothing to pick from the apple, I was willing to do it right then and there. Also, I felt so useless for not being able to get my wife pregnant the old-fashioned way that anything I could do to expedite conception, I would do.

I feel better today writing this than I did after receiving those printed letters from the laboratory. When I read those letters, my soul was crushed. My heart was flattened. It is one thing to be told it will be difficult to have a baby. It is entirely different to be told you simply cannot have a baby. I learned what it felt like to be stripped of hope. If I have a .00000001 chance of getting Nik pregnant through sexual intercourse, then tell me that. Because I will hang my hat on that sliver of daylight, on that .00000001!

I have been pulling rabbits out of my ass for years. I don't intend to stop now.

18
··························

THE GOX-MOHR PROUST
QUESTIONNAIRE

As I finish this book, I'm beginning to feel a combination of the relief and nerves one feels upon completing something one loves but knows will be judged. I was sitting and staring at this damn computer screen one night when my wife thrust a sheet of paper into my hands with a numbered list on it. It wasn't a grocery or "honey-do" list. It was simply a sheet of unanswered questions.

Nik said, "Answer these. Then ask Jackie to answer them. Then ask our dads." So I did. I answered. Then I sat down and asked Jackie all the questions on the list. Next I sent the list off to my dad and Mac. With surprising alacrity, we all answered these questions. I was astonished by how eager we all were to

255

do so. Each of us answered honestly and tenderly. It was as if we were finally asked to take the one quiz we knew we couldn't fail. Most importantly, while taking the quiz, we all got to put some deep-rooted emotions on the table. In this quiz lay the free pass for men to share their softer sides. Some of the answers to this quiz made me giggle. Many of them made me cry.

I discovered things about my father and my son that I never would have guessed. I learned more about my father-in-law through this quiz than I ever would have learned through decades of marriage to his only daughter. Who were these mushy, loving men? And why can't we say these things to each other all the time?

My father loves me unconditionally. He has never told me this to my face but now, through the quiz, I have learned how he feels. My son would be a father the exact same way that I am being a parent. Is he kidding me? Every moment of every day that I'm with him, I think that I can't possibly be getting it right. But I am. Through the quiz, I discovered that I am loved and I am great at giving love.

When I showed all of the answers to Nik, she just smiled at me. I asked her what made her compile the list and why she had me give this quiz to the men I love most.

She replied, "Because I knew you needed it."

Perhaps in the male community it is easier to express our feelings in the form of a questionnaire. Nik confided in me that her questionnaire is just a poor man's version of *Vanity Fair's*

Proust Questionnaire. Nonetheless, I strongly encourage you to take it. Give it to your dad. Give it to your sons and your uncles. Give it to any man or woman in your life that you love and want to know more about. It doesn't have to be a relative. You will be shocked by what you will learn.

And without further ado, ladies and gentlemen, the Cox-Mohr Proust Questionnaire:

Do you think it is ever okay to spank a child? If so, when and why?

_____

_____

What's the hardest thing about being a father?

_____

_____

What is the easiest thing about being a father?

_____

_____

What do you think the main difference is between fathering a son and fathering a daughter?

_____

_____

When should it be bedtime?

_____

When is a good age to explain the birds and the bees?

_____

What do/did you want your kids to be when they grow/grew up?

_____

What is the most important lesson to teach your kid?

_____

_____

_____

In what way do you want to be a different father than your own?

_____

_____

Are you ever done parenting?

_____

How the Cox-Mohr family answers these questions (aka the answers that have changed my life forever):

MY FATHER, JON WOOD MOHR

- On spanking: *Yes. It's okay to spank children to get their attention when they've done something really bad or dangerous. This does not mean "beating." Hand spanking is quite different from using belts, switches, and the like, which were the norm when I was growing up.*

- On being a dad: *Disciplining children appropriately is the hardest part about being a father. Loving them unconditionally is the easiest.*

- Sons versus daughters: *"You can have fun with a son, but you've gotta be a father to a girl." (Soliloquy from* Carousel.*) Actually, sons get more latitude to explore and test. There is a*

259

tendency to be more protective over a daughter. You worry more about what your son will to do someone else; with a daughter you worry about what might be done to them.

- On bedtime: *This depends upon the child's age and general health, but generally around 8 P.M.*

- On the birds and the bees: *With sons, there is no appropriate age. By the time you think you should address the topic, they already have most of the answers. With daughters, I lateral the ball to Mom.*

- When they grow up . . . : *Happy and at peace with themselves.*

- The most important lesson: *The Golden Rule.*

- You versus your own dad: *Be more loving and less demanding of achievement.*

- Are you ever done?: *Never. Children provide a lifetime of love* and *anxiety.*

NIK'S FATHER, MEREDITH "MAG" AVERY COX

- On spanking: Spanking *is an interesting word. There is paddling, there is whipping, there is switching, there are many forms; not all are equal. Spanking seems to be the least harsh. Spanking should be used when there is an impression to be left . . . behavior versus consequences.*

- On being a dad: *The hardest part is knowing when to stop protecting and the easiest part is to care.*

- Sons versus daughters: *In my experience, fathering a son takes significantly more work than fathering a daughter. I would expect early man recognized this when trying to teach hunting/gathering techniques to his son. Make no mistake: it is the mother who has the toughest job of all, though.*

- On bedtime: *Bedtime should be at the end of the day. That is to say, have a routine; but be flexible. As a member of the "early birds," bedtime would usually dictate sometime around 8 P.M. until your child reaches ten years old. After that, it will gradually move toward the natural "end of the day," until control no longer exists at all.*

- On the birds and the bees: *It's an interesting concept to think about how hard it is to explain how birds or bees mate. On the other hand, if you go to the zoo and point at two hippos mating, almost no words are necessary at all. My guess is that most is already known when one actually makes the decision to explain "the hippos." Maybe ten is a good age.*

- When they grow up . . . : *They could be whatever they wanted. I think there was a time when I joked about having a doctor in the family so that medical care was ensured. I may have been on to something then . . .*

- On the most important lesson: *Family, respect, love, and self-confidence. Everything else will come.*

- You versus your own dad: *I don't want to be so different but I think that more open expression of love and support comes easier for me.*

- Are you ever done?: *Yes and no. Yes—you are almost done when your child takes his or her first breath. You are done with life as you knew it before that child's birth, in so many ways. But then no—you are never done until your last breath.*

JON FERGUSON COX MOHR

- On spanking: *No. Spanking teaches your children to fear you. Your kids should respect you. Though as I've said, I've seen other people's kids who could use a good whack.*

- On being a dad: *The hours are tough. It's also hard to trust that you're doing it right and know that they think you're doing it wrong . . . and then realizing that you're both correct. Loving my son no matter what is the easy part.*

- Sons versus daughters: *I think you can make more mistakes with boys. And you don't have to worry which direction they wipe. I only know about raising boys but hopefully in the future, I'll have a better girl answer. (We're accepting prayers.)*

- On bedtime: *Depends on the kid but generally 7:30 or 8.*

- On the birds and the bees: *This also depends on the kid. Some can handle it early (Nik). Some aren't quite ready for it yet (Jackie). Some operate in an alternate universe where you pee in people's butts (me). So for Nik, 4; Jackie, 8; Jay: How does a bird pee in a bee's butt?*

- When they grow up . . . : *I just want him to be happy.*

- On the most important lesson: *Be kind. Be calm. Love hard.*

- You versus your own dad: *I want to be more open about my love—listen more, hug more, kiss more.*

- Are you ever done?: *God, I hope not.*

JACKSON JONES MOHR

- On spanking: *No! Never.*

- On being a dad: *Taking care of a baby because you have to change its diapers.*

- Sons versus daughters: *Girls would want you to buy Barbies but boys would just want cars and* Star Wars *action figures.*

- On bedtime: *7:00.*

- On the birds and the bees: *Right when they learn how to talk.*

- When they grow up . . . : *Really smart, nice guys. I wouldn't want them to be dumb.*

- On the most important lesson: *Just to be nice.*

- You versus your own dad: *I wouldn't be different. I would be exactly like my daddy.*

- Are you ever done?: *No. Forever, even when I am an old, achy man.*

- Bonus Question: What's the difference between a stepmother and a mother? *The mother got married first. That's the only difference. Because they both love me exactly the same.*

Nik and I are both huge fans of the Rolling Stones but one hardly turns to rock stars for wisdom (except for maybe Paul Mc-Cartney or Elvis Costello). But I think that Mick Jagger and Keith Richards really nailed it when they wrote *"You can't always get what you want, but if you try sometimes, well you might find, you'll get what you need."* So thank you, Mick and Keith. Thank you, Jackie boy. Thank you, Dad, and thank you, Daddy. Thank you, Proust. Thank you, Nik, baby. This quiz gave me what I needed.

19
....

NO WONDER MY
PARENTS DRANK

If you're looking for pure, unconditional, unadulterated love to come your way, get a cat. If you are in the market for constant love, caring, and compassion, get a puppy. I say this because if these are your reasons for having children you will be hurt and disappointed and regularly question your own existence.

If, however, you want to *give* those things—put your heart in a child's tiny, dirty hands and make it your job to give and love and give and love and give and love until there is nothing left and then give and love some more—give and love so much that even when your son says he hates you, he never for a moment questions how you feel about him. Then and only then jump headfirst into the murky and turbulent waters of parenthood. The water is cold and can even sting your eyes. But oh, what a beautiful sting it is!

The water is also much deeper than you anticipate. On your best days you're never really touching bottom. But you fake it. You fake it day after day and after a while you build a routine for you and your family and you realize that your kids think your feet are firmly planted on the bottom.

When titling this book, I wanted to express frustration at being a sober parent. I certainly don't want my readers to think it's an indictment on my parents' behavior. My parents weren't a couple of drunks. Only one of them was. But that parent has been sober for over thirty years. It's a shame that drinking while parenting is frowned upon today. Parenting would be so much easier if we could all knock back a couple of apple martinis with dinner. Some of my fondest childhood memories take place in church basements and VFW attics during AA meetings. The place was filled with grown-ups trying desperately to get their lives together. None of them were going to sweat a kid crawling under the pews playing army and trying on choir robes.

"No wonder my parents drank" is a cry of jealousy and enlightenment. No wonder my parents drank. Raising kids is fucking hard. Obviously I am not referring to the kind of drinking that leads to regular beatings. But if Nik and I had a few pops each afternoon, there would probably be a lot less stress in the house.

Haven't you noticed that everything is funny when you and

your friends go out and get hammered? Imagine how much more hilarious our kids would be if we were shitfaced all the time! It would be a blast. All of those half-assed "tricks" that Jackie shows me would be incredible. After I was thoroughly amazed at his ability to stand on one leg, I could then try and break his record. I probably wouldn't quite make it, though, because I'd be drunk (and that, in turn, would please my highly competitive child who needs to win all the time). I would probably tilt over to one side and then list back the other way and fall down. This would also please my child, who loves when Daddy gets hurt. Jackie would laugh hysterically and we would all have a ball. I would no longer get stressed-out about early mornings. If Jackson woke up at 5 A.M. and wanted to play Mario Kart on the Wii, I would make a pitcher of Bloody Marys and join him. We would play for hours and laugh our balls off. I would forget to bring him to school and then we would laugh about that. I think back now at all the times I came home with F's on my report card with notes from my teacher that read "J.J. just doesn't seem to try!" and I understand why my parents drank. Having a smart kid who doesn't try can drive a parent to drink. Fortunately, I have a smart kid who tries. He tries hard.

Nik and I run a pretty tight ship. Dinner is at five every night; followed by the walk with the dog, the bath, the books, and the bed. The problem with running a tight ship is that sometimes your kid wants to stay in the tub too long. Sometimes they just aren't hungry at five o'clock because they had fifteen slices of string cheese on the bus ride home from school. But if I drank,

I wouldn't care. When Jackie says, "I don't want to get out of the tub yet"—hey, no problem. I wasn't finished with my vodka collins anyway. I could go back downstairs and get pie-eyed.

Parents who drink are probably a lot more comfortable with the inmates running the asylum. The absurdity of parenting falls a little by the wayside and they can just kick back with their Stolis and not sweat it. We are all tempted to rub scotch on our babies' gums when they cry. Most of us are also tempted to pour scotch past our own gums and into our stomachs when our babies are crying. But most of us don't.

The earlier generations ruined that for the rest of us. Too many parents would get hammered and forget the basic baby rules like food and water. Too many of our grandpas got drunk and accidentally sat on the baby. Too many of our aunts and uncles got shitfaced and drove us home from school. Too many of our neighbors got loaded and had fistfights on the front lawn in front of all the kids.

Yes, parenting really would be so much easier if we drank. Conversely, smoking grass could make parenting damn near impossible. It would be very hard to get my son out of the bathtub at six-thirty every night if I were sitting in there with him playing with all of his toys. I have met some stoner parents and they seem to have a handle on everything okay but I know that I would be a disaster. It seems like it would be impossible to stop playing Mario Kart if you were baked! You start thinking strange thoughts like, How important is school, really? Or, He can miss a week of school and we'll drive up to the mountains and roll around in the snow. These are horrible ideas. Unless you're stoned. When you are stoned, you have epiphanies like, Holy shit! *SpongeBob* is written for adults! Then you spend the next ten days with your child watching it on a loop.

Stoner parents seem pretty laid-back. They also usually have an odd smell to them. Pay attention the next time you are at the playground and you see a parent who you think smokes grass. They have an odor that is a combination of patchouli oil and ass. You can also spot them easily because their children are all little contact-high stoners rocking back and forth on the swings getting that special tickle in their gut and wearing hemp clothing. Stoner parents' kids are the ones *not* running around. They are usually under a structure drawing in the sand with a stick, under the impression that whatever they are doing under there is some serious shit, because whenever a normal kid runs by, they try to protect their drawing by huddling over it.

You can ask a stoner parent, "Is that your kid over there?" When they say yes and ask, "How did you know?" you can tell them, "Because the kid has been sitting there watching sand fall through his fingers for an hour and a half! For God's sake, smoke in the garage!"

No wonder our parents drank. We never wore helmets. We never came home when we were supposed to. We got stitches weekly. We broke bones annually. We played on the roof of the garage. We got lost. We got lost a lot. We touched each other inappropriately. We didn't try in school. We wrote on the walls. We wrote on ourselves. We wrote on our brothers and sisters. We swallowed pennies. We shit out pennies.

I completely understand why my parents drank. (And thanks for stopping.)

Like all good things, though, childhood must come to an end. At least physically. Nik and I pride ourselves on acting like children together. This is ironic when you consider that our entire day as parents is spent teaching our little one to grow up and act age-appropriate. Little do our children know that after they are asleep, we make silly faces and speak in goofy voices to each other. We even give the dog a strange voice and personality to go along with it and have entire conversations with an animal that has no idea she is even in the game. We do this because it makes us laugh. After everyone is bathed and in their pajamas and the groceries are all put away, Nik and I behave in the child-like manner that is most familiar to us. As grown-ups, we have been unfairly put in charge of other life-forms. It is more work than any of us ever thought we were signing up for but once we are signed up, we do it. We wake up at the crack of dawn to make breakfast. We wake up at the crack of dawn to put school uniforms on our kids. We wake up at the crack of dawn to tell our kids that it is too early to get out of bed.

I finally took Jackie's car seat out of the back of my truck this year. I had no idea that this simple act would make me so sad. Long gone are the days of digging Cheerios out of the crease of his seat. No longer will I wipe down his headrest with paper towels because his juice box sprayed over his head. Like all fathers, I am proud of my son's growth. I have always marked his height on the inside of the closet door in his bedroom. I used to do this on the wall but Mac tipped me to the closet door, the reason being that when you move to another house, you can take the door off the hinges and take the chart with you. I will, Mac. I will.

I hope one day soon my family will need a new house to make room for new babies. I miss cutting grapes in half. I miss stacking pillows up on the living room floor so my kid can sit until he gleefully falls over. I miss cradling my child in my arms. I miss waiting for baby teeth to fall out. I miss the waddle walk and the speech impediments.

The circus is packing up and traveling to another town. It is happening under my nose and right before my eyes. The greatest show on earth is now dressing himself. I sit in the kitchen with my coffee in the morning and he walks down the steps fully dressed for school. He has already brushed his teeth and made his bed without me asking him once. I don't have to change diapers. No longer must I be careful of his eyes. He will never need any of these things ever again. The larger he gets, the smaller his need for my instruction. As he grows, my heart sinks. The less he needs me, the more I need him.

I set the car seat down in the garage on the Thomas the Tank Engine table. I can't bring myself to throw any of this out. In the deepest, brightest parts of my heart, I have convinced myself that I will need all of these things again soon. It's a strange feeling to know that part of your parenting job is over. Now the hard part really starts. Now I have to loosen the reins and let my boy become a part of society.

Recently Jackie and I were in the gas station mini-mart and he looked up and read aloud, "Beverages." Somehow, my son learned to read. This all happened when I *was* looking. In my own house! But . . . he reads? How much longer will he allow me to read to him before bed? I didn't even know how important reading to him was to me but now that he reads on his own, it might be the most important thing to me. The clock is ticking. Tonight I will read to my boy. I will pull out all of my best voices; do my best shtick. I will do all of this hoping against hope that even though he can read, he will like the way I do it better. He won't.

The circus is leaving town. I am now in a race against my own lowly sperm count to bring it back. The question remains, How can I possibly miss it? I've been complaining about it for seven years. I wrote this book about how strange and weird our children are.

But having children *is* the greatest show on earth and I want back in.

I hope that if you are a parent, when you finish reading this little book you will put it down, go to your kids, and hold their faces in your hands. Make sure they hear you. Simply say "I love you." Hopefully they will say "I love you, too." But if you are lucky, and I mean really, really lucky, they will look you in your eyes and say "I know."

ACKNOWLEDGMENTS

I would like to thank Kerri Kolen from Simon & Schuster. Kerri, you worked so hard at putting my rambling thoughts and essays into a workable manuscript. You are not paid enough.

Thank you to Lydia Wills, who told me to get off my ass and start writing this book.

Thank you to Jon and Jeanie Mohr, the parents that borned me, for not leaving me at a night game when I was young. Mom, Dad, I am fully aware how crazy and hyperactive I was as a child. Your patience is greatly appreciated. I love you. I would like to thank Terry and Meredith Cox for creating the most amazing creature I have ever known. Whatever you did worked. Somehow, an entire continent away, you raised my perfect soul mate. Without even knowing me, you made it so we were perfect for each other. I love you.

ACKNOWLEDGMENTS

Thank you, Nik, for being such a constant source of quiet and calm. Thank you for teaching me through example how to be still. You make everything better (especially this book!)

Thank you, Jackie boy. You make me very proud.